THE PACKER TAPES

To Eric:

The smallest
ankle I ever
taped.

Best Wishes

Dom Gentile
"96"

THE PACKER TAPES

*My 32 Years with
the Green Bay Packers*

**By Domenic Gentile
With Gary D'Amato**

Prairie Oak Press
Madison, Wisconsin

Prairie Oak Press
821 Prospect Place
Madison, Wisconsin 53703

Typeset by KC Graphics, Inc., Madison, Wisconsin
Design by Prairie Oak Press
Printed in the United States of America by BookCrafters, Chelsea, Michigan

Library of Congress Cataloging-in-Publication Data

Gentile, Domenic, 1929–
   The Packer tapes: my 32 years with the Green Bay Packers / by
Domenic Gentile with Gary D'Amato
      p.   cm.
   ISBN 1-879483-28-9 (pbk. : alk. paper)
   I. Gentile, Domenic, 1929– .   2. Sports trainers--United States--
Biography.   3. Green Bay Packers (Football team)--History.
I. D'Amato, Gary, 1956– .   II. Title.
GV428.7.G46   1995
613.7'11'092--dc20   95-23837
                                                      CIP

*To a great lady, my wife, who stood by
me through thick and thin during my
thirty-two years as a trainer for the
Green Bay Packers. Margaret raised
the children practically by herself.
We love her very much.*

—Domenic Gentile

CONTENTS

FOREWORD

Numerous books have been written about the Green Bay Packers, but none of them from the unique perspective that Domenic Gentile brings to *The Packer Tapes: My 32 Years With the Green Bay Packers*.

I've known Dom for three decades. He was the Packers' trainer when I played quarterback under Vince Lombardi on the great Glory Years teams and the trainer during my tenure as the Packers' head coach, from 1975 to 1983.

As the team trainer, Dom had to be part healer, part counselor, and part friend. He understood and respected his very important role with the Packers, and never compromised his position.

Coach Lombardi was an exceptional judge of character; that was one of his greatest strengths. When he hired somebody to work for the Green Bay Packers—assistant coach, player or receptionist—that person had to meet the highest standards. Vince hired Dom. That alone says a lot about what kind of man Dom is.

I always thought Dom had the perfect temperament to be the trainer for a National Football League team. He was a keen listener, possessed an exceptional attitude, and was a warm, caring man who brought dignity and integrity to the job every day. In the turbulent and emotional world of professional football, Dom was like the Rock of Gibraltar: strong and steady.

Dom had a great knack for getting players out of the training room and back into the game, but he also recognized when an injury was serious enough to prevent an athlete from performing. He was able to walk that line between management and players, and both sides respected him.

I talked Dom out of suing the NFL in the mid-1970s, when the Packers were fined $5,000 for an alleged illegal dispensation of drugs. Dom was a man of great character. He was proud of his outstanding reputation, and rightfully so. However, at the time, I thought the publicity that would have resulted from a lawsuit would have been unfavorable to the Packers and the League. As far as I'm concerned, Dom never had to clear his name. He was innocent. He presents the facts of the case in this book and in doing so, has attained peace of mind.

This book is loaded with great anecdotes and stories about the Green Bay Packers, seen through the eyes of a man who was privy to locker room banter and coaches' chalk talks.

Domenic Gentile worked with the players. He ate with them, laughed with them, and cried with them.

He was far more than just the team trainer.

He was one of us, and we loved him.

I hope you enjoy his book as much as I did.

Bart Starr

ACKNOWLEDGMENTS

I wish to thank Margaret Meyer, Carol Daniels, Kandi Koehne, Shirley Leonard, Lee Remmel, and Al Pahl for all the help given to us in the writing of this book.

Special thanks to Gary D'Amato for all the great work he has done for this book. Gary traveled many, many miles to meet with me throughout the writing period.

I also wish to thank Kristin Visser and Jerry Minnich, of Prairie Oak Press, for all the help and advice they gave us early on. This book could not have been published without their dedication.

I would also like to acknowledge and honor my family: My mother Ida and my father Dominic (both deceased), my brothers John and Anthony (both deceased); my brother Eugene; my sisters, Esther Schiavetti, Mary Paoli, Edda Olson, and Dora Gentile; our children, Annette Gulseth, Michael Gentile, Gregg Gentile, and Marie Waldschmidt; and our grandchildren, Shane and Dana Gulseth, Chelsea and Taylor Gentile, Allex Gentile, and Ryan Waldschmidt.

INTRODUCTION

One of the first things I discovered about Domenic Gentile was that, after all these years, he still operated on "Lombardi time."

Vince Lombardi, the legendary Green Bay Packers coach about whom the first chapter of this book is devoted, always stressed that if his players were not at least 15 minutes early for a meeting or a practice, they were considered late.

Apparently, Gentile took that guideline to heart.

When we agreed to meet in Green Bay two years ago to discuss the possibility of my writing a book about his career, I made sure to arrive early to make a good first impression.

Dom already was at the designated restaurant when I got there, working on his third or fourth Diet Coke. He glanced at his watch, then up at me, as if to say, "Where have you been?" So much for the good first impression.

At subsequent meetings in Green Bay, Plymouth, and Madison, I tried in vain to beat Dom to the site, usually a restaurant. Each time, I arrived confident that I had gotten there first . . . only to see the big, white Cadillac with the "Domo" vanity plates already parked in the lot. Inside, Dom would be sitting at a table with his notes and newspaper clippings, nursing another Diet Coke.

Punctuality was just one of Dom's virtues. I found him to be a warm and sincere man; a modest, down-to-earth guy with a passionate loyalty to the Packers. He was enthusiastic about the book, always suggesting ideas and strategies.

Dom made it clear from the beginning that this was not to be a "kiss and tell" book, but rather a collection of anecdotes about coaches and players, as seen through the eyes of the team's long-time trainer.

Quite frankly, I wondered if the book would be "meaty" enough to appeal to readers.

But when I began to transcribe the 58 cassette tapes that Dom turned over to me, it quickly became evident that this was a man who knew how to tell a story. His anecdotes were poignant, humorous, and revealing. His recall of details about players, events, and games over the last three decades was amazing. And while there were no character assassinations, Dom didn't hesitate to address such sensitive issues as Chester Marcol's frightening battle with alcoholism or the cracks in Lombardi's armor.

What emerged was a fascinating look at the Packers, written from a unique perspective. I'm confident that football fans, and Packer fans in particular, will have fun reading this book.

I'm also confident that they won't have half as much fun reading it as I had writing it.

Gary D'Amato

THE PACKER TAPES

Chapter 1

Vince Lombardi

Vince Lombardi arrived in Green Bay in 1959, when the Packers were perennial losers but the roster was loaded with future Hall of Famers.

He stepped down as head coach nine seasons and five National Football League championships later, when the Packers were perennial winners but the roster was loaded with aging veterans and soon to be bankrupt of talent.

His timing was perfect.

Like contemporary and friend John F. Kennedy, Lombardi became a legend partly because of who he was and partly because of what he was . . . but mostly because of when he was.

Some people might dismiss this right-place-at-the-right-time phenomenon as historically significant coincidence.

I like to think it was destiny.

In all honesty, Lombardi might not have been as successful in another era, although he certainly would have been a winner in any era. His temper tantrums, his mood swings, his fanatical approach to discipline—even the principles that governed his life and shaped the lives of his football players—would have been oddly out of place in the 1990s. He would not have tolerated the selfishness of many of today's athletes, nor would he have suffered the manipulative agents, the greedy owners, or what he surely would have viewed as a permissive society.

But in the 1960s, in a remote National Football League outpost named Green Bay, coaching a group of athletes who hungered to win but didn't know how, Vincent Thomas Lombardi was the perfect fit.

Although I was a high school teacher and not yet a part of the team in 1958, I remember that the Packers' search for a new coach was pretty exciting because of the names that were being tossed about as possible replacements for Ray "Scooter" McLean, who had compiled a 1-10-1 record in his only season as head coach. Among the candidates were Blanton Collier, the University of Kentucky coach; Otto Graham, the former Cleveland Browns quarterback; and Forrest Eveshevski, the successful coach at the University of Iowa.

Lombardi, the New York Giants' offensive coordinator, also was a candidate. Dominic Olejniczak, then the Packers' president, called Giants owner Wellington Mara and asked permission to speak to Lombardi. Mara was said to be grooming Lombardi to be the Giants' next head coach, so he tried, unsuccessfully, to steer Olejniczak toward another New York assistant named Tom Landry (who, of course, would wind up with the expansion Dallas Cowboys and become a Hall of Famer himself).

The Packers wanted to combine the coach and general manager jobs and were looking for a strong leader. After Eveshevski indicated that he wanted to stay at the college level, Lombardi emerged as the top candidate. Ultimately, the Packers made him an offer: $36,000, for the dual roles of coach and general manager.

After Vince was signed, sealed, and delivered, people throughout Wisconsin were asking the question, "Who the hell is Vince Lombardi?"

They were about to find out.

My association with Lombardi and the Packers organization began in 1961, when I applied for the position of part-time team trainer. At the time, I was teaching history, coaching basketball, and serving as the athletic trainer and athletic director at West De Pere High School in the Green Bay suburb of De Pere.

Carl "Bud" Jorgensen was the Packers' trainer, and he also worked during the off-seasons as a salesman for Bertrand's Sport Shop in Green Bay. He called me one day and said, "Doggone it, Dom, I need an assistant. I know you do the taping and work with the high school kids here. Why don't you call coach Lombardi and tell him you're interested in helping out?"

Since Lombardi oversaw all aspects of the football operation, including the hiring for all positions, I faced the unnerving prospect of having to interview with him.

Perhaps "audition" would be a better word. He asked a few questions, but I felt he was paying more attention to my mannerisms and my expressions than he was to my answers. To be honest, he was not the kind of guy who made you feel at ease. And he had the same fire in his eyes, sitting behind his desk and talking about the part time trainer position, that he had just before kickoff on Sunday afternoons.

Whatever it was I said or did, I apparently passed his test. It probably didn't hurt that, like Lombardi, I was a Roman Catholic of Italian descent.

At any rate, after about five minutes he smiled and said, "Well, I think you're my man." Our handshake began my 32-year career with the Packers organization.

In my first minicamp, Jorgensen had to leave town for a few days, and I was responsible for taping all the players before practices. On the second or third day, Lombardi made an appearance in the training room to take a look at the newest addition to his staff.

Jorgensen had suffered an accident while he was in high school and had lost the second finger on his left hand. Still, he was one of the finest tapers I ever saw, and I tried to emulate him. But with Lombardi watching over me like a hawk, I was extremely nervous. Beads of sweat rolled down my forehead and palms. I fumbled around and dropped a roll of tape.

"You know what your problem is, young fella?" Vince said, sizing me up. "You've got too many damn fingers."

He roared with laughter, and his joke helped break the ice. From that point on, I was much more relaxed, and my taping improved 100 percent.

Lombardi was everything that has been said and written about him, and more. Depending on your viewpoint, he was either a simple man with simple values and beliefs, or he was a complex human being. He could be abrasive or charming, volatile or introspective, combative or unassuming, profane or articulate.

As Jerry Kramer, the Packers' great right guard, once said: "Vince is a cruel, kind, tough, gentle, miserable, wonderful man whom I often hate and often love and always respect."

Lombardi's coaching philosophy was amazingly simple. He knew the game came down to just two things: blocking and tackling. The team that mastered those two fundamentals and was properly conditioned would win more games than it lost.

"If a man is running down the street with everything you own, you won't let him get away," he would say. "That's tackling."

And so, he drilled the Packers until they could block and tackle in their sleep. Sloppy execution in either was, in his eyes, an unpardonable sin.

"You will make mistakes," he would tell his players, "but not many, if you want to play for the Green Bay Packers."

His philosophy on life was just as simple: Integrity and pride were at the heart of character, and character was at the heart of success.

Armed with those beliefs, Lombardi turned a talented but directionless group of athletes into one of the greatest dynasties in the history of professional sports.

In his nine seasons, the Packers won 98 games, lost 30 and tied 4 for a winning percentage of .758. Green Bay also won five NFL championships, the first two Super Bowl games, and the hearts of fans nationwide.

And I got to go along for the ride.

Lombardi was a great judge of talent and character, but above all else, he was a master psychologist. He knew that it took no special talent to diagram plays on a chalk board. In order to make those plays come to life, however, he knew he had to be able to get inside his players' heads and, more importantly, their hearts. He motivated the Packers by appealing to their pride.

And he used whatever means necessary to accomplish that objective. He pleaded, screamed, cried, challenged, urged, threatened, ridiculed, cajoled, and demanded. Sometimes it was an act, and sometimes it wasn't. Only Vince knew the difference.

I'll never forget when Paul Hornung came back after being suspended by the NFL for the 1963 season for gambling. We were playing an intrasquad game early in training camp, and Hornung got the ball on a sweep. He drifted wide, waited patiently for the blocking to set up and then made a perfectly timed cutback. No defender laid a hand on him, and he scored on a 20-yard run.

Vince turned and yelled, loud enough for the entire team to hear, "Hornung's back! Hornung's back! The Golden Boy is back!" He was like a kid at Christmas.

It was a great bit of psychology. He was telling the players that all they had to do was block and tackle and they'd be back in the championship race.

One year, late in the season, Vince went out and bought 80 wool shirts for the team. There was nothing special about them, but Vince called them "super shirts" and said they would keep the players warm and give them better freedom of movement under their pads. Vince started wearing his super shirt to practice and pretty soon all of the players were wearing them.

Regardless of how cold it was, the players would wear only their pads, pants, jerseys and the super shirts. It got to the point where they really believed the super shirts were keeping them warm, and they forgot about the weather and concentrated on playing football.

We used those shirts for several years, until new, better-insulated underwear came along. And I'll tell you, during the super shirt era, we didn't lose very many games.

Sometimes, Lombardi's motivational technique was a bit more harsh.

In 1965, we were coming off our second successive second-place finish in the NFL's Western Conference. Second place, in Lombardi's eyes, might as well have been last place. "Hinky-dinky," he called it, and it might have sounded funny if he didn't spit out the syllables as if they were poison.

We had gotten off to an 8-2 start, but on Nov. 28, the Los Angeles Rams whipped us, 21-10, in Los Angeles. With just three games left in the regular season, it was the sort of loss that could have deflated us.

Lombardi wouldn't allow that to happen.

On the Tuesday after the game, he called a team meeting in the locker room. He was so angry his face was dark, almost black, and that was not a good sign. In those days, there was no door between the training room and the locker room, so I heard every word that was said.

Lombardi started by questioning defensive end Lionel Aldridge's manhood, because Lionel had made the mistake of singing on the flight home from Los Angeles. Soon, he was lashing the entire team. Although his tirades were laced with profanities, this was one of the rare times that I heard him take God's name in vain.

"Goddamnit, you guys don't care if you win or lose!" he screamed. "I'm the only one who cares. I'm the only one who puts his blood and guts and heart into the game. You guys just show up. Listen a little bit, Goddamnit! You've got the concentration of three-year-olds. I'm the only guy who gives a damn."

He ranted and raved for what seemed to be an hour, but probably was no more than four or five minutes. Suddenly, there was a stirring in the back of the room, a clatter of chairs. And as the players turned around, they saw tackle Forrest Gregg on his feet, bright red, with a player on either side, holding him back by the arms as he strained forward.

"Goddamnit, coach," said Gregg, who also seldom swore. "Excuse the language, coach, but it makes me sick to hear you say something like that. I want to win. It tears my guts out to lose. We lay it on the line for you every Sunday. We live and die the same way you do, and it hurts."

Tackle Bob Skoronski jumped to his feet. "That's right!" he yelled. "Damnit, coach. Don't you tell us that we don't care about winning. That makes me sick. It makes me want to puke."

By now, the other players were nodding agreement and murmuring and saying, "Yeah, that's right, coach."

It was unanimous. The Packers were ready to prove the old man wrong, or die trying.

Needless to say, we went on to win the Western Conference championship that season, then we beat the Cleveland Browns, 23-12, in the NFL championship game.

Lombardi had gotten the desired effect with his tantrum. I'm fairly certain that it was not a spontaneous outburst, but rather a well-planned speech, complete with staged emotions.

Of course, not all of Vince's tirades were planned. In training camp before the 1966 season, he was emphasizing pass protection because he felt Bart Starr had been hurried into too many poor throws the year before.

One day, his voice hoarse from yelling, Lombardi lost his temper and ran onto the field to confront Steve Wright, a huge, good-natured tackle from Alabama who was having trouble with his blocking assignments.

Lombardi flailed away with his playbook, smacking Wright over and over in the chest. Wright just stood there, shocked, until the coach calmed down.

"I guess I was trying to get him to hate me enough to take it out on the opposition," Lombardi said later. "To play this game, you must have that fire in you. And there is nothing that stokes that fire like hate. I'm sorry, but that is the truth."

Once, the Minnesota Vikings were driving against our defense in a game at old Metropolitan Stadium. They scored an apparent touchdown on a pass play, but Vince ran up and down the sideline, screaming, "Interference! Interference!" Apparently, one of the officials had seen the offensive pass interference, too, because he threw a flag.

In those days, the players from both teams stood on the same sideline at the Met. Norm Van Brocklin, the Vikings' coach, thought Lombardi had influenced the official to make the call. Van Brocklin screamed at Lombardi, "Nice call, you fucking dago."

Vince, of course, was extremely upset about the slur, but he didn't say anything. However, after the game—which we won—he threw a tantrum in the locker room, calling the Vikings a bunch of crybabies. He became so worked up, he almost passed out. Packers Hall of Famer Tony Canadeo, then one of the team's radio broadcasters, had to calm him down and bring him into the training room to sit down.

Another sore point with Lombardi was the Thanksgiving Day series with the Detroit Lions. He detested any variation from his routine, and playing on Thursday was exactly that. Also, it was always a road game for the Packers. One year, we had the lead at halftime and were warming up for the second half when the field's sprinkler system suddenly came on. Lombardi was afraid the turf would get muddy and hamper our running game. He whirled and shook his fist in anger at the press box, where William Clay Ford, then the Lions' president, was sitting. It was almost comical.

Every day during training camp, Lombardi, a devout Catholic, attended 6 a.m. mass. It was my job to awaken training camp visitors, who were strongly urged to attend mass and take communion with him. If by chance a visitor overslept, his chances of being invited back to camp were slim.

Vince believed that those early morning masses helped him control his temper at practices. But he still had plenty of explosions left in him, and I certainly witnessed a number of them over the years. It is a bit disconcerting to imagine that his temper could have been worse than it was.

Sometimes, the smallest things set him off.

During training camp one year, I had painstakingly punched out all the players' names in plastic tape and put the neat strips above the respective lockers. Lombardi came in, saw what I had done and had a fit.

"What the hell is that?" he barked. "We don't need that stuff. Take it down!"

I think he was upset because the locker room had been renovated and he didn't like too many luxuries for the players. He didn't want them to get soft. For some reason that I still don't understand, he viewed the plastic tape as a luxury.

When Vince had his game face on, nobody messed with him. Nobody even talked to him. Once, we were on our way to a game at County Stadium in Milwaukee on buses we took from the old Astor Hotel. Vince Lombardi Jr. was sitting next to me, near the front of the bus. Vince was sitting in his customary seat at the front of the bus, on the right side.

"Hey, dad, you know you're wearing my socks, don't you?" Vince Jr. said innocently.

Vince just glared at him and said, "Son, one of these days you're going to talk too much."

In the late 1960s, Ed Sabol of NFL Films put together an outstanding documentary that chronicled Lombardi's career. Sabol was unsure of one scene in which Vince clearly vented his anger on the sideline after the Los Angeles Rams blocked a punt late in the game that led to a 27-24 defeat in 1967.

"Should I take that scene out?" Sabol asked Vince.

"Absolutely not," Lombardi answered. "Let it go."

The scene stayed in, but after the film was screened at a press conference, one of the reporters wasn't satisfied.

"Was the film cleaned up, coach?" he asked Lombardi.

"What do you mean, 'Cleaned up'?" Lombardi snapped.

"You know," the reported stammered, ". . . the language."

Vince shouted back at him, "I never use foul language, mister. I have never used foul language in my life."

Well, Vince was exaggerating a little bit. But in truth, he used expletives much less frequently than most people think, even on the practice field.

His temper, however, was legendary.

Pete Rozelle, then the young commissioner of the National Football League, often was the target of Lombardi's rage. It is a little known fact that Rozelle and Lombardi not only did not see eye-to-eye on many matters; they simply didn't like each other. I think Rozelle feared Vince because many people felt Vince would have made a great commissioner. And Vince thought Rozelle could be compromised, which to Lombardi was the equivalent of being a worm.

Once, Vince called me into his office while he was on a conference call with Rozelle and members of the Lions front office. They were arguing about a player who was trying to get out of his contract in Green Bay. Rozelle sided with the player, who ended up going to Detroit.

Vince was absolutely livid. He was shouting into the phone, chastising the Lions executives and fuming at Rozelle.

"Pete," he yelled, "that's a very gutless decision you just made. You're letting a player run this league. I'm going to tell you right now, Pete, don't you ever come to Green Bay again!"

Lombardi ended the conversation abruptly by slamming down the phone.

And you know, throughout the 1960s and all our championship seasons, Rozelle never once visited Green Bay. He never watched a game at Lambeau Field. But on the very night that Vince left to take the head coaching job with the Washington Redskins, Rozelle flew in and gave a speech to the B'nai B'rith. Coincidence? I don't think so.

Lombardi was not an easy man to work for because he was so gruff and demanding, and so stingy with praise. But I think I earned his respect over the years.

During my first training camp, Tom Bettis, one of our starting linebackers, was nursing a sore knee. The coaches wanted him back on the practice field, but I knew that there was something seriously wrong with the knee—it was swollen and made a clicking sound when he flexed it. I suspected cartilage damage.

I was not in a position to get too pushy, but I told Tom that I thought he needed surgery. Lombardi became furious when he found out what I had done and confronted me. Somehow, I found the fortitude to tell him that I thought the knee would get worse if Bettis didn't have the surgery.

Vince finally calmed down and said, "It was good that you made those observations. I think you're going to be good for the Green Bay Packers."

A few years later, Bart Starr was practicing on a bad hamstring. It was bothering him to the point that his movement was impaired. After about a week, I went up to Vince and said, "Coach, he's got to get out of there and rest because he's got a hamstring and it's only going to get worse."

Vince didn't even look at me. He just yelled, "Bart Starr, get off the field!"

Once, a player came into the training room with some cysts on his back, and they were seeping. I wasn't sure what they were, but I knew enough to send him to the hospital, because if what he had was contagious it would spread like wildfire throughout the team.

At practice the next day, Lombardi asked Bud Jorgensen where the player was, and Bud said he didn't know.

"Well, who the hell does know?" Lombardi said.

"I do, coach," I said. "I sent him to the hospital."

I explained the player's condition and Vince was not happy.

"You mean you sent him to the hospital for that?" he said.

I told him I was afraid the condition might be contagious and that we shouldn't take any chances.

He thought about that for a moment and said, "Makes sense to me."

As volatile as Lombardi was, though, he had a soft side. Jerry Kramer likes to tell the story of when he was a second-year player, going through Lombardi's first training camp with the Packers. Lombardi had been riding Kramer mercilessly for several days, telling him that he ran like a "fat cow" and suggesting that he go home to Idaho.

Finally, Kramer had had enough. He sat in the locker room after a particularly grueling practice, his spirit crushed, and thought about quitting.

Lombardi saw Kramer hanging his head and sensed, correctly, that he had pushed the talented young player to the brink. He approached Kramer, mussed his hair and said softly, "Son, one of these days, you're going to be the greatest guard in the league."

It was the right thing to say, and at precisely the right time. At that moment, Kramer would later write, he would have run through a brick wall for the old man.

One year, an undersized but determined defensive back named Joe Scarpati tried to catch on with the Packers. Lombardi loved Scarpati's hustle and attitude, but the team was loaded with great defensive backs such as Willie Wood, Herb Adderly, and Bob Jeter.

The day Scarpati was informed that he would not make the team—and I'll never forget this as long as I live—he came down to the practice field and begged Lombardi to keep him on the roster. He said he'd play for nothing; he just wanted a chance to play for Vince.

Lombardi told him, "Joe, I could put you on our taxi squad, but with your talent, you should be playing somewhere."

Scarpati started to cry, and it was somewhat embarrassing. Finally, he composed himself, shook Lombardi's hand and walked off the field.

I know Vince felt compassion for the kid. He walked over to me and said, "Dom, that's the tough part of this business. But it's the best thing for Joe. To have him sit around on the taxi squad would have robbed him of a valuable year of experience."

Scarpati wound up going to Philadelphia and had a fine seven-year career. He still ranks sixth on the Eagles' career interception list with 24. He also played one year for New Orleans, and on Oct. 8, 1970, he was the holder when the Saints' Tom Dempsey kicked his record 63-yard field goal.

As usual, Vince was right.

While I'm on the subject of Vince's softer side, there's something else few people know about him: He had a wonderful, self-deprecating sense of humor. He enjoyed a good joke, and you could hear his laugh across a crowded room. It came from the belly, a deep guffaw that made his eyes dance and exposed those crooked, white teeth.

I remember once when our equipment manager, Gerald "Dad" Braisher, went into Lombardi's office to have him sign a purchase order. Vince was not in a good mood.

"What the hell is this for?" he demanded.

"It's a purchase order," Braisher said. "We're out of toilet paper."

"The hell with toilet paper," Vince said, throwing the papers back at Braisher. "We don't need any toilet paper."

Well, the next day Vince came into the office and went to use the rest room. He found strips of newspaper had been cut and laid neatly over the toilet paper dispenser, which was empty. He roared with laughter.

When Paul Hornung's gambling suspension ended, Lombardi ordered him to come to Green Bay so he could supervise Hornung's off-season conditioning program. Hornung, as one might guess, was not in great shape. One day, I was giving him an ultrasound treatment after he had pulled a groin. A young sportscaster from New York named Howard Cosell was in town to interview Hornung, and we were all in the training room when Lombardi walked in.

"Coach, how many great sportscasters do you think there are?" the late Cosell asked Lombardi in that measured nasal twang that was to become famous years later on "Monday Night Football."

Vince shot back, "One less than you think, Howard." I don't think Cosell was amused, but Hornung nearly reinjured his groin, he was laughing so hard.

Once, Vince couldn't move out of the way of a pileup near the sideline during a game. Ray Nitschke came roaring in to make the tackle and his momentum carried him into our bench, where he bowled over Lombardi, whose glasses and trademark hat went flying. When the players saw the play during the film session the following week, they howled with laughter.

"Run it back, run it back!" they yelled.

Vince ran the projector back and forth several times. He let the players have a good laugh. Finally, he became irritated and said, "OK, let's get serious now."

Lombardi was not above crying in public, either. When we beat the Rams, 28-7, in Milwaukee in 1967 to win our third consecutive Western Conference title, Vince started into his post-game speech but broke off in mid-sentence, choked with emotion. With tears streaming down his cheeks, he knelt and led the team in the Lord's prayer.

Once, I was telling Vince about my mother, Dora. Mom never watched Packer games on television or listened to them on the radio. Instead, during the games, she would go upstairs, sit on her bed and say the rosary over and over, praying for the Packers and their Italian coach. As I finished telling the story, I glanced at Vince and I swear I saw tears in his eyes.

For all his success, I suspect Lombardi never managed to shed the thin layer of insecurity that he had wrapped under years of self-discipline. Perhaps because of that, he was extremely distrustful of the media. He never volunteered information to reporters, and when he was asked questions, he was guarded with his answers.

One day the phone rang in the locker room and it was Chuck Johnson, a reporter for the *Milwaukee Journal,* hoping to ask Vince a few questions. I approached Vince and told him that Johnson was on the line.

"What the hell does he want?" Lombardi barked.

I said, "Coach, Chuck does a pretty good job covering us. He hasn't written anything negative that I know of."

Lombardi turned and said, "I want to tell you something after I'm done talking to him."

About five minutes later, he came back and said, "These reporters, they're all buddies when you're winning. But let yourself slip once and they'll cut your throat, no matter how nice you've been to them."

Lombardi did everything he could to make himself unapproachable to the media. He was consistently rude and abrupt in his dealings with reporters. The writers who covered the Packers in those days had a grudging respect for Vince, but I'm certain they never really warmed up to him. Bud Lea of the *Milwaukee Sentinel* once told me, "Vince had better not ever lose."

And, of course, he didn't.

If you haven't guessed by now, Vince had a huge ego. But surprisingly, it was very easily bruised.

For example, he was irritated when the city of Green Bay started talking about changing the name of City Stadium to Lambeau Field in 1965. He didn't like the idea. Curly Lambeau, who had died on June 1 of that year, was a legend in professional football, and particularly in Green Bay. Call it jealousy, but I don't think Lombardi wanted any part of further glamorizing Lambeau. He really fought that name change. Some people said it was because he wanted the stadium to eventually be renamed "Lombardi Field." I'm not sure about that. I do know that he wanted to have total control in Green Bay; I'm not only talking about the football franchise, but in many cases, city politics. The name change did go through, of course, and he was not happy about it.

It was one of the few times that he did not get his way in Green Bay. For all practical purposes, Vince was the team owner. He had total control of the football operations; over who went with the team on road trips; over salaries and hiring and firing; and, yes, over even the purchase orders for toilet paper. He made all the decisions, because he felt that was the best way—the only way—to run the franchise.

Vince was a dictator, but you have to remember that he had been turned down for several head coaching jobs until he got his opportunity in Green Bay. The Packers job was his first big break, and he wasn't going to allow anybody else to mess it up for him.

In fact, Vince was responsible for changing the way the franchise was run. When he came to Green Bay, the team was governed by a board of directors that numbered about three dozen. It was an unwieldy number and Vince was uncomfortable working with that many people. He demanded that the board elect a seven-man Executive Committee. Period. That Executive Committee, in consultation with Lombardi, would run the franchise. Technically, those seven Executive Committee members were Lombardi's bosses, but I'm not so sure it wasn't the other way around.

To this day, the Green Bay Packers operate exactly the same way; the corporation is governed by a seven-person Executive Committee elected from a 45-person board of directors.

Not only did Vince rule with an iron fist, but he ruled with a tight one, as well. When he came to Green Bay, the Packers had $250,000 in the bank. That's all there was. And Vince didn't like to spend it. He was so frugal, he wore the same cap until it practically had holes in it. He couldn't bear to throw his caps away, so he would give them to the trainers or the equipment men, making a production of it as if he was passing on a rare and valuable gift. Little did he know. I still have one of Lombardi's original caps, and it's priceless.

Emlen Tunnell, a great defensive back whom Vince had acquired from the New York Giants, borrowed ten dollars from the old man during training camp one year. Every day, Vince would remind Emlen about the debt. One day, Emlen was in the training room when Vince came in to talk to me. On his way out, he said, "And don't forget, Emlen, you owe me ten dollars."

Emlen said, "Coach, how can I forget when you remind me every day?"

Vince was tight, but he wasn't irrational about it.

The week before Super Bowl II, we practiced in Green Bay—despite sub-zero temperatures—because Vince wanted to save hotel money by waiting until just a couple of days before the game to fly to Miami.

On the Tuesday before the game, the thermometer dipped to minus 10. We were on the practice field for about 15 minutes, when I noticed that Lombardi was getting white spots on his earlobes. He was wearing a wool cap, but he hadn't pulled it down over his ears.

So I kind of sauntered over to him and said, "Coach, I think you're getting some frostbite on your ears."

He looked kind of startled. He blew his whistle and yelled for Tom Miller, officially the assistant to the general manager and unofficially Vince's right-hand man.

"Get on the phone," he told Miller. "We're going to Miami right now."

He got everybody off the field, and we went straight to the airport. He hated to spend that extra money, though.

Everybody knows the story of Lombardi's first encounter with a sports agent. Jim Ringo, our Hall of Fame center, had hired a representative one year in an effort to get a big raise out of Lombardi. Instead, Ringo got a big shock. The agent came to the Packer offices and introduced himself to Vince, who immediately excused himself from the room. After a few minutes, he returned and said curtly, "I agree that Jim deserves a raise, but you're talking to the wrong man. Mr. Ringo is now the property of the Philadelphia Eagles."

Later, when the upstart American Football League started competing with the NFL for players, salaries skyrocketed. Vince had to shell out a lot of money for Donny Anderson, his first-round draft pick in 1965, and Jim Grabowski, his first-round pick in '66.

The next year, one of our players was speaking at an off-season banquet in Milwaukee when he turned to Vince and said, jokingly, "How does it feel to be the third-highest-paid member of the Green Bay Packers?"

Everyone in the room laughed except Vince, who stared straight ahead. He was not amused.

When the Packers started winning, Vince relished his status as a national celebrity. He liked people to know that he could pick up the telephone and call George Halas, or Pete Rozelle, or even President Kennedy, whom he had supported in the Wisconsin primary.

Lombardi always kept his downstairs office door open, and anyone within earshot could hear his conversations. Since the training room was close to his office, I often was within earshot.

In 1961, I overheard Vince ask President Kennedy for a favor. Kennedy granted it, and that favor helped us win the NFL championship. This is a true story that very few people know:

Paul Hornung, our Hall of Fame halfback, was in the Army that year, stationed at Fort Riley, Kansas. Ray Nitschke and Boyd Dowler also had been called up by the Army, but all three played games that season on weekend furloughs.

However, as the historic 1961 NFL championship game approached, Hornung discovered that Fort Riley had split its two-week Christmas furloughs. Those whose last names started with the letters "A" through "H" would take the first two weeks. That meant Hornung would have to be back at Fort Riley for the second two weeks of vacation, and would miss the Dec. 31 game against the New York Giants.

"I called coach Lombardi," Hornung later told me. "I told him that I had gone through the ranks and talked to my sergeant and my captain and everybody at the base to see if I could get my two weeks switched with someone else. The answer was, no way. They said they couldn't do it.

"Coach Lombardi told me, 'You just be ready to go.' I've got President Kennedy's phone number, and he always said if I ever needed anything to call him. Well, I'm going to call him."

Sure enough, Lombardi called Kennedy's private number at the White House and Kennedy immediately picked up the telephone. I listened as Lombardi explained to the president of the United States that he needed Pvt. Paul Hornung's services for the NFL championship game.

Lombardi concluded the conversation by saying, "I would appreciate anything you can do, Mr. President. God bless you, Jackie, and the kids."

Within minutes, Kennedy was on the phone to Fort Riley. One can imagine the shock of some colonel picking up the phone and hearing: "This is President Kennedy calling. There is a private on your base named Paul Hornung. I want you to do me a favor and get him out of his second two weeks of his duty so he can be in Green Bay, Wisconsin. I don't think that's too much of an imposition. We can handle this, can't we, colonel?"

Hornung said he was on the plane back to Green Bay before the colonel even delivered the pass. "So, if it were not for coach Lombardi's relationship with President Kennedy," he concluded, "I would have missed the game."

Hornung had a pretty decent day, too. He scored 19 points—an NFL record—on a touchdown, three field goals, and four extra points. He also rushed for 89 yards and caught three passes. We beat the Giants, 31-0, in the first league championship game played in Green Bay.

Another one of Vince's friends was General Douglas MacArthur. When Vince was an assistant coach at Army, one of his duties was to take the Saturday game films to MacArthur's suite at the Waldorf Astoria in New York City for a private viewing.

In 1962, we were to play the Giants in the NFL championship game in New York. Vince knew that I had taught high school history classes, so he invited me to join a small group of people who were to visit the great general in his suite. I was extremely excited.

Unfortunately, MacArthur took sick and the meeting never took place. It was one of the most disappointing days of my career.

Vince took advantage of his status in other ways. There is no doubt in my mind that one of the reasons we made so many great decisions on draft day in the 1960s was that Vince got tips and inside information from the numerous college coaches who visited Green Bay to observe training camp practices.

Vince invited the college coaches to his "Five O'Clock Club"—an informal social gathering before dinner at St. Norbert College—and it doesn't take a genius to figure out that one of the topics of conversation was that year's top college prospects. Scouting was not nearly as scientific then as it is now, and those talks undoubtedly gave Lombardi an edge on draft day.

By the mid-1960s, the Packers were winning championships, and Green Bay was a wonderful place to live. But all was not right with the "outside" world. The counter-culture was emerging, led by militant extremists and people such as Jerry Rubin and Abbie Hoffman. By 1967, they were imploring their followers to "burn the flag, burn churches, burn, burn, burn."

To Vince Lombardi, it was easy to lump together the Yippies and hippies and radicals and perceive in them a united front against the values he cherished.

Lombardi simply could not understand how they could break the law and defy authority. I think that hurt him on a personal level. One day he came in the training room and the radio was blaring about the rioting and the Yippies and hippies. He whirled and slapped it, and it flew across the room and smashed into the wall. Lombardi walked out of the room, muttering to himself. The radio was mine, and Vince never did pay me for it.

Vince apologized for being so slow to recognize the danger in the youth revolt. He said he had been so wrapped up in the Packers, he had not been attentive to the problem.

"It is becoming increasingly difficult to be tolerant of a society that has sympathy only for the misfits, only for the maladjusted, only for the criminal, only for the loser," he said in a widely quoted speech. "Have sympathy for them. Help them. But I think it's also a time for all of us to stand up and cheer for the doer, the achiever, one who recognizes a problem and does something about it, one who looks for something extra to do for his country—the winner, the leader."

Race relations also were turbulent in the 1960s. It's no secret that many NFL teams were affected by strained race relations, but the Packers were not one of those teams, and Lombardi was the reason. Skin color didn't mean a thing to Vince. The only colors he saw were green and gold. Anyone who wore a Packers uniform was a member of the family. His family.

Still, it was not easy being a young black man in Green Bay, which was and still is populated overwhelmingly by whites. Lombardi did not duck the issue; he encouraged all of his players to think and talk about race issues. He stressed that his office door was always open; if a player had a problem, he could go directly to Vince. And he constantly reminded them to focus on their goals.

One year, Vince planned to participate in a Wisconsin autumn tradition: Deer hunting season. The black players got together and bought an orange vest, the kind deer hunters wear. They drew a big target on its back and placed it in Vince's office. When he saw it, he laughed so hard, tears came to his eyes.

Of course, it was inevitable that Lombardi would burn out. Few men could put as much into their jobs—physically, mentally, and emotionally—as Lombardi poured into the Green Bay Packers. And there is little doubt Vince recognized that he had gotten all he could out of the team. The timing was right. So on Feb. 1, 1968, Lombardi stepped down as coach, retaining his title of general manager.

"You know, the pressures of losing are bad," he told close friends. "But the pressures of winning are worse, infinitely worse, because they keep on torturing you and torturing you."

Lombardi named Phil Bengtson, whom he had hired away from the San Francisco 49ers when he arrived in Green Bay, as the Packers' new head coach. Phil was a great guy and a brilliant defensive coordinator, but he had to fill the biggest set of shoes in NFL history. And to be fair, he did not have the kind of raw, young talent at his disposal that Lombardi had in 1959.

It wasn't long, however, before Vince realized that he had made a mistake. He missed coaching, missed it terribly. He was such a restless person during the 1968 season; it was almost a pity to watch him. He would come out to practice, stand around with his hands behind his back and watch—sometimes for a few minutes, sometimes for an hour. Often, he would sidle up to me and say, "Is the team ready, Dom? Are the guys ready to play football?" He was uncomfortable, and I was uncomfortable for him.

Vince walked through the locker room one day after we had lost a couple games in a row. Colored dress shirts were just coming into vogue then, and Jerry Kramer was wearing a crisp new blue shirt and a tie.

"You know what the trouble with this team is?" Lombardi said to nobody in particular. "We have too many blue shirts around here."

Kramer came into the training room after Lombardi walked out and said, "Well, it looks like the old man has me pegged for out of here."

Kramer stayed, but things didn't get much better. After we finished with a 6-7-1 record, our first losing season since 1958, Vince could have fired Phil and taken back his coaching job. Nobody, probably not even Phil, would have objected. But Lombardi would never even consider such an act of disloyalty to a friend.

The only way Lombardi could get back into coaching, in his eyes, was to leave Green Bay. The inevitable happened on Feb. 6, 1969, when he accepted an offer to coach the Washington Redskins.

Before he left, Lombardi pulled me aside and said, "Dom, I'd like you to come with me to Washington."

I had wondered, many times, what Lombardi thought of me as a trainer. He was the kind of guy who never really went out of his way to be nice to people. Believe me, compliments from Vince were rare. When he gave one, it meant something. His offer was a tremendous compliment, and I was both stunned and flattered.

I had never even considered the possibility of Vince asking me to go with him. "I'll have to think about it for a couple of days," I told him.

"Well, you go home and think about it, but I need your decision in a day or two," Vince said.

I went home and talked it over with my wife. We had four children, and she wasn't crazy about the idea of uprooting the family and moving to Washington. To be honest, neither was I. So I went back to Vince and told him that I couldn't take him up on his offer.

Had I been young and single, I would have jumped at the chance because of the tremendous respect I had for Vince. At least I can take it to my grave that the greatest coach in NFL history wanted to take me with him to Washington.

The last time I saw Vince in Green Bay, he was standing in the lobby just outside the ticket office. He seemed at ease, and maybe just a little pleased with himself. He stopped to talk with me, and in those few short minutes, I saw a side of him that I had never seen. He expressed gratitude for all the things that people in the organization had done for him. He was warm and compassionate.

I sensed I could tease him a little, so I said, "Coach, now don't go over there and do what you did here."

He smiled a bit and got a faraway look in his eyes.

"Oh, no," he said, "what happened here will never happen again."

Vince autographed a photograph for me that day. It read, "To Dom, my trainer. Cordially, Vince Lombardi." I still have it.

The Redskins, like the Packers before Lombardi's arrival/revival, were a sorry bunch. They had gone 5-9 in 1968 and had managed to put together 14 consecutive losing seasons. Since their last league championship in 1942, they had a record of 126-190-15.

In their first year under Lombardi, the Redskins went 7-5-2. Vince was viewed as a messiah of sorts in Washington. It is not an exaggeration to say that his press conferences drew as many reporters as President Nixon's.

Tom Brown, who played for Lombardi's Packers and briefly for the Redskins before retiring, told me years later that Vince was not the same person in Washington as he had been in Green Bay. Tom said that Vince had more patience with the Redskins and that he rarely raised his voice.

I had always felt that Vince's biggest strengths were his abilities to motivate and teach. I didn't think he needed to be quite as vociferous in his approach in Green Bay. And obviously, he saw the need to change with the times. That flexibility was another strength. Vince could and would change to stay a step ahead.

During a game against the 49ers in October of the 1969 season, several people on the sideline noticed Lombardi clutching his abdomen. In the heat of battle, this could be dismissed as a nervous stomach. But by June 1970, he began having digestive problems that could not be ignored. On June 27, Vince underwent an operation in which two feet of colon were removed.

It was announced that a tumor had been found but that it was not cancerous. That was not the truth, of course, but Lombardi did not want to alarm his father, who was old and ill.

I can't help but think that an injury Vince had suffered many years earlier, when he was a member of Fordham University's "Seven Blocks of Granite," may have ultimately contributed in some way to his illness. During a scrimmage, Vince had been kicked in the abdomen and suffered a separation of the duodenum, a section of the small intestine. The injury caused internal hemorrhaging, and Vince was carried off the field and placed in the infirmary. Incredibly, he showed up on the field the next day and attempted to practice. He collapsed again, went back to the infirmary, and played little the rest of the season. One has to wonder if his effort to come back too soon didn't cause unseen problems that would someday lead to cancer.

When I visited Vince in the hospital, it was obvious that he was a very sick man. The cancer had spread quickly, despite cobalt treatments. He probably had lost 40 or 50 pounds. He was gaunt and pale.

"I can fight anything, Dom," he said, "but this is a battle I just might lose."

Few people knew then that Vince was not happy in Washington. He and Marie wanted to return to Green Bay, and Vince had had discussions with some members of the Executive Committee to that effect. But a triumphant return to Titletown was not meant to be.

In one of his last official acts, a gravely ill Lombardi attended the league meetings in New York and gave an impassioned speech to the owners, who were facing new labor issues and problems. Lombardi stood up and said something to the effect of, "Don't let a bunch of snot-nosed kids take this league away from you."

Death came on Sept. 3, 1970.

"The power of Vince Lombardi's personality swept the world of sports," President Nixon said as he led a nation in mourning. "When I think of him standing at the side of a football field, his attention focused on the field . . . he was an imposing figure, and an inspiring one. On the field and off, his very presence was commanding. As I think of him that way, I know that he will always hold a place in the memory of this nation.

"Vince Lombardi believed in the strength of a nation, through its playing fields. He believed in his church, his home, his family, and his team. Lombardi built his life around basic values, and that is why his greatness as a coach was more than matched by his greatness as a human being."

I paid my own way to be at Vince's funeral at St. Patrick's Cathedral in New York. I wanted to touch his coffin, to hug his wife and son, Vincent Jr., and daughter, Susan.

It was Labor Day weekend, but several thousand New Yorkers stood behind police barricades to watch. I was standing with several Packers players, waiting to go into the cathedral, when a huge black man appeared out of nowhere. He was blind and had a cane, and somehow he had wound up in an area restricted for players and family members.

I approached him and asked him if he needed help. He explained that he had taken the bus from Georgia to be at Vince's funeral. He didn't know Vince, had never even met him, but he had two boys who were athletes and he had raised them by the Lombardi creed: Hard work, dedication, perseverance. He said it was his hope that his sons become good athletes and great citizens. I am sorry to this day that I did not get his name.

When it was time for the players to go into the cathedral, I took him by the arm and guided him in with us. Unfortunately, the seats were reserved, and I realized he would have nowhere to sit. But in one of the pews across the aisle, a woman motioned for me to bring the man over; there seemed to be room for one more person. She was so gracious. She couldn't do enough for this man. After the service was over, I watched her take him by the arm and lead him out of the cathedral. She got him a cab to take him to the bus station.

The woman was Ethel Kennedy, the widow of Bobby Kennedy. (Vince, it turns out, had occasionally escorted Ethel to functions in Washington, and the two were good friends.)

I think that story, more than any other, illustrates Vince Lombardi's charisma and influence. His life, and what he stood for, crossed all social, economic, and ethnic lines. He was a great man. I was in awe of him then, and I am in awe of him now.

Once again, I must defer to Jerry Kramer, who summed it up so well after our 33-14 victory over the Oakland Raiders in Super Bowl II:

"Perhaps we're living in Camelot. Many things have been said about coach Lombardi, and he is not always understood by those who quote him. But the players understand.

"This is one beautiful man."

The following are a few of my favorite Lombardi quotes:

"Football is a symbol of what's best in American life. A symbol of courage, stamina, coordinated efficiency and teamwork. It's a Spartan game, a game of sacrifice and self-denial, a violent game that demands discipline seldom found."

"Heart power is the strength of the Green Bay Packers. Hate power is the weakness of the world."

"The test of this century is whether we mistake the growth of wealth and power for the growth of strength and character."

"Dissent is good. It's a form of articulation. But destruction is anarchy. Problems cannot be solved by waving the American flag, but neither can they be solved by tearing down or burning the American flag, breaking windows, and kicking in doors. This country has many problems. The thing to do is to solve them sensibly."

"People shout to be independent while at the same time they are dependent. They also condemn authority while at the same time requiring the exertion of authority by their own actions. We must walk a tightrope between the consent we can achieve and the control we must exert."

"The struggle America faces today is a struggle for the hearts and souls and minds of man. Unlike football, where there are millions of spectators but only a few players, the struggle is a game where there are no spectators but where everyone is a player."

Chapter 2

Introductions

Nothing in my past had prepared me for my job as the Green Bay Packers' trainer, unless you count the fact that I taped the ankles of young athletes during my years as a high school teacher and coach.

How I came to share the sideline with every Packers coach from Vince Lombardi to Mike Holmgren, and along the way work with such great players as Paul Hornung, Ray Nitschke, Bart Starr, James Lofton, and Sterling Sharpe . . . well, it still seems like a dream.

I was born on Jan. 28, 1929, in Hurley, Wisconsin, a small town at the northern edge of the state.

Hurley was an iron ore mining town, and the Great Depression really hit the area hard. My father, an Italian immigrant, was unemployed for much of my childhood, and in those days there was no unemployment compensation. Dad was a very proud man and he refused to accept relief of any kind. I vividly remember the orange pick-up truck that went around the neighborhood, dropping off grapefruit, oranges, apples, and even steel-buttoned shirts to needy families. The pick-up always skipped the Gentile house, because my father wouldn't accept the help.

With eight children in the family, there were never any presents under the Christmas tree. And it was just as well, because there was never any tree. We couldn't afford one until I was 16 years old. We would all hang up stockings, and dad would put 10 or 15 cents in each. Some years, it was just a few pennies. Unfortunately, he would take the money back on Christmas Day, because we needed it for food.

I remember many meals at which dessert was a lone apple, cut into 10 pieces. A lot of kids raided gardens to be mischievous in those days; the Gentile kids did it to survive.

When I was in the second grade, we couldn't afford to buy those little boxes of Valentine's cards that kids exchange in school. While everyone else in my class was passing cards back and forth, I scrunched down in my desk and tried to hide. It was a humiliating experience, and I've disliked Valentine's Day ever since.

Somebody told me that smoking cigarettes would curb my appetite, so I would follow people who were smoking on the street and wait for them to discard the butts, hoping all the while that they wouldn't stomp on them.

My older brother John and I wore the same size clothes, and there were times when we attended school every other day, alternating because we had to share pants and shirts. Toilet paper was a luxury we couldn't afford; we used cut-up newspapers or paper bags. Shoes were hard to come by, too. I remember wearing a pair of high-top rubber boots every day, winter and summer, for two years.

We couldn't afford to go to the dentist, and I suffered from toothaches throughout my childhood. I can't tell you how many times I was scolded in school for "inattentive behavior" because I sat with my hands on my chin and didn't do my work. I was afraid to tell the teacher that I had a severe toothache. This went on until my sophomore year in high school, when my family finally was able to arrange a payment plan with a dentist.

When it came to medical treatment, we were a bit luckier because the only doctor in town also happened to be the mayor of Hurley. He would treat our family, and in exchange we would help him during re-election time by putting up signs and distributing literature.

I took a job as a paperboy for the *Duluth News Tribune,* and the income, albeit small, helped our family tremendously. I did well with the route and steadily increased my customer base. But one day, a wealthy family on my route accused me of stealing a half-pint of cream from their milk box. Of course, the paper fired me. Three months later, they caught the guy who stole the cream, but I never did get my job back.

When World War II broke out, my father went down to the train station every day to see off the young men who were entering the service. Unfortunately, he didn't get to greet many of those soldiers when they returned. Dad died of cancer at 62 in 1945.

My mother couldn't go out and get a job because she didn't speak English. By the time I started my senior year of high school, however, our family was doing a little better financially. I was working at a gas station, earning $9.90 a week, and trying to save for junior college. Two of my sisters, Esther and Mary, had jobs, and John was in the service and was sending money home. The Gentile family's income for 1946 was $1,462.80.

I had been a pretty good athlete in high school, making the all-conference teams in both football and basketball. At Gogebic Community College in Ironwood, Michigan, I made the all-conference football team both my freshman and sophomore years. Then it was on to North Dakota State in 1949, where I played end as a junior and again made the all-conference team.

During the summer months those years, I worked the graveyard shift, 11 p.m. to 7 a.m., for the Hurley police department. Since I was not a full-fledged policeman, I was not allowed to carry a gun.

One night, Ralph Capone, who lived in a small town south of Hurley, came staggering out of a downtown bar. He wasn't a gangster, like his infamous brother Al, but he liked to project the image. For instance, he would send in his two bodyguards to check out a bar before he entered. It was just for show, but it was pretty damned impressive.

Anyway, Ralph was stone cold drunk, and his bodyguards were nowhere to be seen. He walked to his car and started fumbling with the keys. I approached him and asked for the keys, telling him he was in no condition to drive. He started yelling at me, and I hollered right back. Finally, I said, "You are not going to drive this car. Period."

Ralph came to his senses and said, "OK, I give in. I won't drive the car. I'll get a hotel room and stay overnight." His car keys had fallen on the seat, so I picked them up. I noticed two rolls of silver dollars, and I handed them to Ralph.

A few days later, I received a nice note from Ralph, thanking me for not letting him drive. And he sent along the silver dollars, with instructions to use them for spending money in college.

In my senior year at North Dakota State, I tore both the anterior and posterior cruciate ligaments in my knee. In those days, reconstructive knee surgery was the stuff of science fiction, so my budding football career was over.

I was a bit depressed and running out of money, but one of my college professors encouraged me to continue my education and helped me get a job at the Elks Club in Fargo. I was a drink runner. The pay wasn't great, but there were always 50 or 60 card players in the card room, and they usually tipped well.

In 1951, I decided I wouldn't wait for graduation in June because the Korean War had broken out. I thought it would be to my advantage to volunteer for the service, rather than wait to get drafted. But I was concerned about finishing college. I went in to talk to the university president, and he said, "Don't you worry about it, Dom. You're close enough to finishing that we can waive some things."

About a month into basic training, a big envelope arrived for me. It contained my college diploma.

I was stationed at Fort Bliss in White Sands, New Mexico, and was just about to enter officer's training when I reinjured my knee during bivouac. I had to walk two miles to a medical facility the next day, and from there I was taken to a discharge center, where I was given $40 and a handshake. I had served only 88 days.

I returned to Wisconsin and landed a job at Rudolph High School for the princely salary of $2,900 a year. I celebrated by buying a car in 1952; not only was it my first car, but it was the first automobile owned by any member of the Gentile family.

I spent two years at Rudolph, then I moved on to Chilton (Wis.) High School, where I taught history and coached basketball. We had a 7-11 record my first year, which was almost like winning the state championship considering the team had lost 36 consecutive games before I got there.

In 1954, I accepted a job at West De Pere High School in De Pere, Wisconsin. I taught and coached basketball for nine years, and also served as the athletic director and trainer. It was that experience that led to my job as trainer of the Green Bay Packers.

Years earlier, when I had interviewed with the principal at Rudolph, he told me about a young man named Darrell Reber who lived a mile from the school but had dropped out early in his senior year. Darrell was a good athlete, but he had quit the basketball team the year before after a run-in with the coach. The principal asked me if I would try to talk Reber into finishing his education.

I walked over to the Reber farm, and I found Darrell out in the field on a tractor. He told me he didn't like school, but he didn't look thrilled to be up on that tractor, either. He was plowing, but I didn't see a whole lot coming up except rocks and dust.

We talked for a while, and finally he said, "If I come back to school, what am I going to do about makeup work?"

I knew I had him.

"We'll take care of that," I said.

Darrell did come back, and he wound up being an excellent basketball player. After he graduated, he asked me, "Now what am I going to do?"

"I know what you're going to do," I told him. "You're going to go to college."

"You've got to be kidding me," he said. "No way."

I called Chuck Bentson, the basketball coach at North Dakota State, and told him about Reber. "He's got a good shot, and he plays pretty good defense," I said. "I don't know if he can play on the collegiate level, but he's worth a look."

"Send him up," Bentson said.

Darrell went to North Dakota State and made the basketball team. But about a year later, he got involved in the Air Force ROTC and was bit by the flying bug. He became a pilot, and flew many years for Northwest Airlines. He made a lot of money and moved to Seattle, where he built a beautiful home and a big stable to board horses.

Eventually, I fell out of touch with Darrell. I didn't talk to him for a period of 12 or 14 years. Then one day, out of the blue, he called and said he wanted to send Peggy and me to Hawaii for a two-week vacation. And he insisted on giving us $1,000 spending money.

"You turned my life around 30 years ago," he told me. "This is my way of repaying you."

I was flabbergasted, and at first I didn't want to accept his generous offer. But some of his friends assured me that Reber was a millionaire, and that I would be disappointing him if I turned him down. So we went to Hawaii, and we had a wonderful time.

I didn't have much when I was growing up. But, like Darrell Reber, I have a lot to be thankful for now.

Chapter 3

Aches and Pains

Nelson Toburen made the tackle, but he didn't get up. His screams sent an icy chill through me as I ran onto the field.

Johnny Unitas, the great quarterback of the Baltimore Colts, stopped me before I got to Toburen.

"Is your orthopedics guy here?" he asked.

I nodded and he said, "You'd better get him out here. Your guy just broke his neck. I heard it pop."

It was Oct. 8, 1961. We were playing the Colts in Green Bay, and it was just my fourth game as the Packers' assistant trainer. Welcome to the NFL, I thought.

Toburen, a rookie linebacker from Wichita, had tackled Unitas as the quarterback scrambled on a broken play. Nelson had lowered his head at impact—the cardinal sin of tackling—and had absorbed the full blow of Unitas' thigh on the top of his helmet.

The force smashed Toburen's chin into his chest, breaking his neck.

I was the first to reach him. He was lying on his stomach, and it didn't take a medical genius to determine that he was experiencing horrendous pain.

Dr. Eugene Brusky, our team physician, and Dr. Jim Nellen, the Packers' orthopedic surgeon, quickly joined me and helped roll Toburen onto his back.

In those days, we didn't have the portable neck traction units that are now attached to stretchers. So, instinctively, I grabbed Toburen's chin with one hand, and, with my other hand under his helmet, I pulled his head straight back to take pressure off the break.

When I did that, Toburen felt no pain at all. But after a couple of minutes, I started to get arm cramps, and Nellen took over for me. As long as one of us maintained that pressure, Toburen felt fine. Any decrease in the pressure, however, and he started screaming.

The tricky part was getting his helmet off. I was able to slip my scissors between the jaw pad and the helmet structure itself, and I popped the jaw pad loose. Finally, we slipped the helmet off his head.

But there was still the matter of getting him off the field. I took turns with Nellen pulling back on Toburen's chin as we rolled him toward the locker room. When we got there, we cut a slit in a towel, slipped it over his head and pulled on both ends. We used that makeshift traction unit all the way to the hospital.

Toburen underwent surgery, and his football career was over. It was a shame, because he was a terrific young player. Several weeks after the operation, he flew with the team to a game. I was sitting next to him on the airplane when coach Vince Lombardi came back, patted him on the cheek and said, "Nellie, you would have been one of the greatest. We're going to pay you off. We don't want you to play football again."

Today, Toburen is a successful attorney in Wichita Falls, Kan. You'd never know, to look at him, that he suffered a very serious neck injury on the football field more than 30 years ago.

In the three-plus decades that I served as the Packers' trainer, Toburen's broken neck was the scariest injury I saw. And I saw plenty, too, from dislocated limbs to broken bones, from torn muscles to shredded knees.

My 32-year association with the Packers spanned seven coaching staffs and 494 National Football League games. I taped approximately 325,000 ankles in my career, and it's safe to say I gave 225,000 treatments of one kind or another.

I guess that qualifies me as an expert on the subject of injuries in professional football. They are as much a part of the game as touchdowns, field goals and nickel defenses.

During a seven-year career, the average NFL player will be involved in 130,000 collisions in games and practices. The properly conditioned human body is an incredible machine, but it simply is not built to withstand that many violent collisions.

An athlete can concentrate on conditioning, nutrition, strengthening exercises and proper technique all he wants, but inevitably, if he plays football long enough, he will get hurt. That's a fact.

"Almost no one leaves this game unscarred, either physically or mentally," says Miki Yaras-Davis, the director of benefits for the NFL Players Association. She's right.

As the Packers' trainer, my job was to get injured players back on the field as soon as possible. Along with the team doctors, I determined when they were healthy enough to play, without jeopardizing either the team's chances to win or their careers. Sometimes, it was a difficult line to walk.

I can honestly say that only once did I have a serious confrontation with a coach who questioned my judgment. Chester Marcol, our outstanding kicker throughout the 1970s, had torn a muscle in his kicking leg one year. One of the assistant coaches impressed on me the need to get him back on the field. Unfortunately, a torn leg muscle does not heal in two or three days. It takes weeks.

We treated Chester aggressively, but the leg did not respond as fast as the assistant coach wanted it to. He kept insisting that Chester should be out on the field, doing some kicking.

Finally, I got a little burned, and I took Chester and the coach onto the practice field. I set up the ball about 15 yards from the goal post, a mere chip shot for him under normal conditions. But these were not normal conditions. Chester swung his right leg feebly and the ball never even made it to the cross bar.

The coach stopped pestering me about Chester.

In many cases, however, it was the player who wanted to get back onto the field before he was ready. After all, playing in pain is part of the deal. In the ultra-competitive world of professional football, those who can play with injuries have an edge over those who cannot.

Lombardi certainly believed that if a player was not seriously hurt, there was no reason he could not perform up to the coach's high standards. But contrary to popular myth, he never, ever jeopardized a player's health or well-being by making him play with a serious injury.

Lombardi believed strongly in taking precautions when it came to injuries. He had a rule that every player had to have his ankles taped for all practices; if you were caught without your ankles taped, it was a $150 fine. In the 1960s, when most players were making $25,000 or $30,000, that was a lot of money.

Lee Roy Caffey, one of our starting linebackers, didn't bother getting his ankles taped for a light workout the day before a game against the Minnesota Vikings. Sure enough, he sprained his ankle.

Lombardi came over and said, "Lift up your sweats and pull down your socks, Lee Roy." He saw that there was no tape.

"OK, Lee Roy," Lombardi said, "that'll be $150."

The next morning, we were at the stadium, getting ready for the game. Lee Roy was sitting on the training table, his ankle swollen and an ugly shade of purple. There was no way he was going to play that day.

Lombardi walked in, took the ice bag off Caffey's ankle and studied it for a few seconds.

"Well, Lee Roy, I'll tell you what," he said. "If you play today, the fine will be rescinded."

Caffey didn't hesitate. He looked straight at me and said, "Tape up." He went out and played the entire game.

Something similar happened to Ron Kostelnik. Kos suffered a knee injury during training camp of his rookie season in 1961. Looking back now, I'm sure he had at least a partial tear in his anterior cruciate ligament. He couldn't practice, and Lombardi was losing patience.

One day he came into the training room to talk to Bud Jorgensen and me about Kos.

"We're going to have to get rid of this guy unless he starts practicing," Vince said.

When Kostelnik hobbled into the training room later, I told him what Lombardi had said. He got up off the table and went out and practiced. We had to do a heavy tape job on his knee every day for the rest of his career. It's amazing how players can overcome injuries when their jobs are on the line.

Getting back to Caffey, he was pretty tough, but he wasn't what I would call a conditioning fanatic. In fact, few players in the early 1970s were aware of the benefits of what is now commonly called aerobic exercise. Some teams were just beginning to stress cardiovascular fitness at that time.

I had read about a doctor at the University of Wisconsin named Bruno Bahlke who was at the forefront of the fitness movement. Bahlke had trained the German ski patrol during World War II, and it was a documented fact that his skiers were able to maintain a heartbeat of 200 beats per minute for up to two hours.

Zeke Bratkowski and I drove to Madison to interview Bahlke. He guaranteed us that he would be able to improve our players' level of fitness by 30-40 percent. He came to Green Bay and set up a grueling running program that consisted of alternating long and short sprints.

Caffey wasn't crazy about the program. The first day, he was sucking for air as he ran past Bahlke. He stopped and gasped, "Hey, doc, now I know why you Germans lost the war—you were too damned tired to fight."

Even when the situation is much more serious than a conditioning drill, a sense of humor is a valuable tool. Whenever I went onto the field to assist an injured player, I always tried to crack a little joke or say something to lower his anxiety level.

Occasionally, it worked in reverse. I've always loved the story, supposedly true, about Paul Hornung getting knocked out in a game while he was at Notre Dame. When he came to, the trainer was standing over him with smelling salts.

"How do you feel, Paul?" he asked anxiously.

"I feel OK," a groggy Hornung replied, "but how's the crowd taking it?"

No injury is a joking matter, but the point is, it's important to remain calm and positive. Believe me, on many occasions my perceived nonchalance was an act. The player is worried enough; he doesn't need a jumpy trainer trying to help him. So I always tried to say something to keep both of us loose. And no matter how bad the injury was, I always tried to find some comforting words. For instance, if a player suffered a broken fibula, I would say something like, "Thank God it's not the tibia," a more serious break.

I figured that if I could convince a player that his injury was not as bad as he feared and that everything was going to be all right—even if I had my doubts—it was an important first step in his recovery.

One of the things that amazes me about NFL players, as a rule, is their unusually high pain threshold. Quarterback Lynn Dickey dealt with pain nearly every day of his career, yet he was able to go out onto the field and perform. Lynn's problems—and you'll be reading more about them later in this book—started with a hip socket that was virtually blown apart when he was with the Houston Oilers. He was damaged goods by the time the Packers picked him up in 1976. The next year, he suffered a broken left leg, and he didn't fully recover from that injury until midway through the 1979 season.

When Lynn broke his leg, doctors operated to insert a plate to help the bones heal. They cut him a second time to insert a steel rod in the leg. Finally, they operated again to remove the rod. In between, he suffered from acute tendinitis.

The doctors can tell you all about those operations and procedures in clinical terms. I saw the other side of it; the human side. As Lynn's trainer, I worked extensively with him during the agonizing period between the scalpel and his return to the playing field.

I have never seen anybody quite like Lynn. We put him through a torturous rehabilitation program that had no precedent. There were no guidebooks to follow on this one. Lynn didn't even have enough strength to lift light weights; the tendinitis in his patellar tendon and other areas of his left leg had left him extremely weak. Finally, we rigged up a homemade device: We set up a chair on the training table and used a strap, hooked to a chain, to help him lift the weights.

It was agony for him. The feeling around the locker room was that he would never take another snap, and I know there were an awful lot of times when he must have wondered, "Why the hell am I doing this? Why am I putting myself through this pain?"

But knowing Lynn the way I do, I don't think he ever seriously thought about quitting. And sure enough, he had several productive seasons for the Packers after that.

I can think of dozens of other examples of players who performed in pain. Dave Hanner, a defensive lineman in the 1950s and early '60s, was fashioning a homemade shin protector from a tape can before a game once and the knife he was using slipped and slashed his leg.

He called the team doctor over and said, "Stitch this up."

The doctor said, "Well, we can stitch it up, but you might as well take your uniform off. There's no way you're going to play today."

Hanner, with a big old chaw in his mouth, just spit and said, "We'll see."

Hanner played. By the end of the game, his right pants leg, stocking and shoe were drenched in blood. He didn't miss a single play.

A few years later, Hanner had an appendicitis attack on a Friday. He went into the hospital, had his appendix removed and played the following Sunday—nine days post-operative.

Ken Bowman, our center from 1964 to 1973, was another player who was able to perform at a high level despite chronic pain from numerous shoulder separations. Vai Sikahema returned punts for the Packers with a separated shoulder and a pulled groin in 1991. That same year, Bryce Paup tried to play against the Chicago Bears despite a pulled calf muscle that made it difficult for him to walk; he didn't want to come out of the game, and I eventually had to advise the coaches to pull him.

Sterling Sharpe played most of the 1990 season with three fractured ribs. Most fans who watch the games on Sunday would never go to work on Monday with three fractured ribs. That season, Sharpe caught 67 passes for 1,105 yards and six touchdowns.

Somehow, these athletes are able to summon the inner strength to keep competing. They willingly subject their injured bodies to additional physical punishment that impedes the healing process. And it's not always the medicine and the ultrasound treatments that keep them going; often, it's just something that comes from within.

A nose tackle came to Green Bay from the Indianapolis Colts in the pre-season in 1988. He was only 26 years old, but he was suffering from a degenerative disk condition and had undergone reconstructive surgery on his shoulder two years earlier. He had once remained in a game after dislocating both of his shoulders, and he lived in constant pain. He paced his use of painkillers so that he would not develop a dependency.

We put him through rehabilitation, but we could see almost immediately that his condition was not going to improve, so we released him before the season started.

I asked him if he thought football had been worth the sacrifice.

"I don't regret a thing," he told me. "If I had a chance to do it all over again, I'd do it the same way."

His story is a sad one, but by no means is it atypical in the National Football League.

Jim Otto played 210 consecutive games over a 15-year career with the Oakland Raiders. Twelve times, he made the American Football League All-Star team or the NFL Pro Bowl team. He once was the league's "Iron Man," but now he's the man of steel—steel screws, steel plates, and a few plastic parts thrown in. Otto has had 16 knee operations—five of them to implant artificial knees—and two major back surgeries.

Former Raiders offensive lineman Curt Marsh, who retired in 1987, had his right foot and lower right leg amputated on Sept. 21, 1994. Marsh played seven seasons with the Raiders; he was hospitalized 18 times and had 13 surgeries. His worst injury, the one that ultimately led to the amputation, was a broken ankle during training camp of his fifth season that went undetected. He took more than 100 painkilling shots and continued to play.

Said Marsh: "They told me if I took the shots and played, it would get better."

I don't know if Otto and Marsh were advised to retire by the Raiders' trainers and doctors. I can't speak for that organization. But if I had a player who had, say, multiple knee surgeries, I would sit him down and say, "Listen, somewhere down the line, you are going to pay for this. There is no doubt you are going to have an arthritic condition in that knee. You will not be able to walk normally. Now, if you're willing to accept that, fine. But my advice to you is to get out of the game."

Players like Otto and Marsh probably would not have heeded that advice.

Miki Yaras-Davis believes she knows why football players are able to play through pain and injury, and why many prolong retirement. Yaras-Davis claims that for many players, football is an addiction.

"The psychology is the same as people addicted to alcohol or drugs," she said. "It gives them a high. The mind-set is, 'I know I pay a high price for this addiction.' But they're still going to keep on going. And when it's over, they're still going to say that football was the best part of their lives."

A National Football League Players Association (NFLPA) survey conducted in 1990 found that of the players leaving the game because of injury, 70.6 percent said they had emotional problems during the six-month transitional period after football. Of those who did not leave because of injury—which in most cases meant they were released by their teams—56.2 percent reported similar emotional problems.

Also in the NFLPA survey, 82 percent of retired NFL players had ailments that they believed were the result of their pro football careers. Some faced surgery to repair or replace joints that no longer worked properly. Arthritis was a common complaint, which came as no surprise. A few reported impaired hearing or vision. Some said they ached so much, they couldn't even toss the football around with their children in the backyard.

The survey indicated that 67 percent of the players had suffered a "major" injury during their playing days; that is, one that caused them to miss three or more consecutive games. Furthermore, 34 percent suffered two or more such injuries.

About 51 percent of the players who answered the survey said they have had problems since the day they retired. Another 12 percent said 10 or more years passed before they experienced problems (usually degenerative arthritis).

Sadly, the number of serious injuries in the NFL is increasing. I can recall very few Packers from the 1960s who suffered knee injuries that required surgery; today, knee injuries involving torn cartilage and shredded ligaments are commonplace.

The simple reason is that bigger, stronger, faster players make for more violent collisions. The average weight for a lineman on the Baltimore Colts championship teams in 1958 and '59 was 240 pounds;

today, the average NFL lineman tips the scales at 300. Other factors in the escalation of injuries are artificial turf and steroid abuse.

And let's not forget another important reason the numbers have gone up: Unlike the 1960s, when players often didn't report minor injuries, every injury today must be reported by a player to the team trainer. It's a stipulation in every NFL contract. Unreported injuries can jeopardize a player's workman's compensation and impact his salary and insurance. So everything gets reported and documented. Some of the things that players reported to me in the 1980s and '90s would have been laughed at 20 years earlier. But it's a good rule.

People often ask me if I am alarmed at the number and severity of injuries in the NFL. Every injury is unfortunate, but to be honest, there is nothing surprising about those NFLPA numbers. Football is a brutal game, one that glorifies violent collision. I don't mean to be cold about it. It's just a fact. Furthermore, every player who enters the NFL fully understands the risks. These guys do not answer the telephone or push papers for a living; they have been conditioned to hit and be hit. And in the NFL, they are compensated very well to do just that.

Now, that doesn't mean the league should be satisfied about the injury situation. There is plenty of room for improvement.

Quarterbacks often are on the receiving end of serious injuries. Since they are the NFL's marquee players, one would think the league owners would be extremely protective of them. True, the "in the grasp" rule and stricter enforcement of unnecessary roughness have helped, but more can be done.

I know some people already believe that there are too many officials on the field, but I'd like to see the NFL add a second referee in the offensive backfield, specifically to protect the quarterback. Currently, the lone referee has to watch for holding, illegal head slaps, unnecessary roughness . . . I just don't think one official back there is able to do what the rules are asking him to do.

I would like to see a second referee added who would have a different sounding whistle, or perhaps a horn, that he would sound to indicate to defensive pass rushers that the play is over. Because, let's face it, after the quarterback releases a pass, there is no need for any collision that involves him.

Of course, you'd have to sell the quarterbacks on this idea, too. I remember when the "in the grasp" rule was passed, our own Bart Starr kind of laughed about it and made the comment, "What'll be next? Pink dresses for the quarterbacks?"

Another way to cut down on quarterback injuries would be to make rib protectors mandatory. The rib pads would protect the quarterback from blind side hits and also would help when he is in the vulnerable position of releasing a pass.

Unfortunately, many players—and especially quarterbacks—are reluctant to wear any extra protective equipment. They believe that just a few more ounces of equipment will restrict their mobility.

Starr didn't wear a rib protector until late in his career. There was nothing on the market at that time, so we devised a flak jacket for him to wear. It was made of a hard plastic, and it is now displayed in the Packer Hall of Fame. The jacket weighed only about 8 or 9 ounces, but Bart thought it was too heavy, so we eventually came up with a cloth vest that was lined with plastic inserts. It looked like a bandolier.

David Whitehurst, one of our quarterbacks in the mid-1970s, refused to wear a rib protector during his final season with the Packers. He paid the price, suffering severely bruised ribs.

It's no secret that foot, ankle, and knee injuries increased dramatically with the advent of artificial turf. I wish the NFL had had the foresight 20 years ago to fund its own research and come up with a turf shoe that reduced the risk of injuries. Unfortunately, the research was done by the shoe companies, and it was done by trial and error. I'll never forget the season we lost 11 players to knee injuries of varying degree. What a waste.

Turf shoes are much better today, but they still can't prevent every injury. The shoe that does probably cannot be made, but the NFL should continue to strive for that goal.

Finally, the NFL can continue to legislate against dirty play. Stiff penalties and big fines have helped reduce the number of cheap shots that are taken. Dirty play definitely is on the decline. But in any business, a few people will always try to play outside the rules, so it's imperative for the league to continue to enforce its rules. It's important for the players to have respect for the game and for one another.

Ultimately, though, football will never be a "safe" game. There is no rule that could have prevented the paralyzing injury that Detroit's Mike Utley suffered in 1991. Utley slipped off his block and fell, landing helmet-first on the turf and damaging his spine. It was an unfortunate, freak accident.

The only way to eliminate injuries would be to change dramatically the way the game is played.

But then it no longer would be called football.

Chapter 4

Pills and Chills

Chester Marcol suffered a groin pull during practice the week before the Packers' game against the New York Jets on Nov. 4, 1979. He insisted on playing in the game, so we injected him with a local anesthetic called Marcaine. Our team doctors had obtained samples of Marcaine, a new painkiller, from St. Mary's Hospital in Green Bay.

Chester went out that day and kicked, but he did not perform well and in the process he re-aggravated the injury. He was ineffective the rest of the season, and the next year was released by the team.

The parting had less to do with his slipping performance and his injuries than it did with his drug and alcohol abuse. Despite our attempts to rehabilitate him, Chester was an out-of-control user by 1980, heavily into narcotics, hallucinogens, and alcohol.

That fall, a reporter tracked him down in a tree stand in the middle of the woods during Wisconsin's deer hunting season. Frustrated and scared and no doubt feeling sorry for himself, Chester told the reporter that the team had tried to cover up his groin injury in 1979.

The reporters ran to me, and I told them the truth: Chester had insisted on playing against the Jets, and since we knew he would play, there was no reason to report the injury to the league.

Well, the story was all over the newspapers the next day, and of course the NFL got wind of it and was concerned about the publicity. So the league conducted its own "investigation," and I use that term loosely.

The NFL dispatched a couple of officials to Green Bay. They interviewed me on the practice field about Chester and the Marcaine injection. Marcaine was a drug that had not yet been approved by the league, even though it was being used in hospitals.

These guys talked to me for about 10 or 15 minutes, and it became clear that they were on a mission, that they had an agenda to follow. I told them that if they would follow me, we would go find Dr. Brusky and straighten everything out. They refused.

A few days later, the NFL announced that it had cleaned up its little mess in Green Bay and had fined the Packers. The amount of the fine was not revealed, and although it was not a huge amount—$5,000—it was the principle that counted.

Domenic Gentile was the convenient scapegoat. Fine the trainer, and the league looks good in the eyes of the public. The NFL is policing this drug thing, by God.

Obviously, my reputation didn't matter to the NFL. But it mattered to me. I had always tried to do the right thing, to be honest and forthright. I had four children in school, and they had to put up with taunts about their daddy injecting people with nasty, secret drugs.

I was so mad, I wanted to sue the league. Bart Starr, who was the coach at the time, talked me out of it, saying that the publicity would be bad for both the Packers and the NFL.

I didn't give a damn about the league but I didn't want to do anything that would hurt the team, so I agreed not to pursue a lawsuit.

The irony of the whole thing made me sick. The Packers were so far ahead of the NFL when it came to drug-testing that Pete Rozelle should have been ashamed and embarrassed.

The league, at that time, did not require the recording and reporting of the dispensation of medications to individual players. They just wanted aggregate team totals. Does that tell you something about the NFL's drug program?

Three years earlier, in 1977, I sat down with Starr, Bob Harlan—our corporate general manager at the time—and the team attorney, and we decided that it would be to our advantage to maintain more detailed records of the dispensation of medications. From that day on, any medications given to our players had to be by individual prescription.

As far as drug-testing, we had been doing that since the early 1970s. We found some problems; some we solved, some we got rid of. It would be nearly two decades before the NFL would invoke random drug-testing in 1990—and only after the huge steroid scare. Negative publicity, right?

I would be lying if I said that drugs were never a problem in the NFL, and it would be foolish to say that the problem has been totally eradicated.

In the old days, players used amphetamines to jack themselves up. Later, they used anabolic steroids to bulk themselves up. Among recreational drugs, alcohol has always posed the biggest problem, but marijuana use escalated in the 1970s, and in later years cocaine reared its ugly head.

If you're serious about your career, you stay away from that stuff because it can only hamper your performance.

Steroids are another problem altogether, because they are known to increase strength, muscle definition, and aggression. And football players, like other athletes, are always looking for an edge.

I read a story about a doctor in California who polled 100 world-class athletes. He wondered whether they would take a drug that was guaranteed to improve their performances, even if 50 percent of them would die using it. Every single one of the athletes was willing to take the risk.

I first noticed steroid use among a few of our players in 1970. These guys had gone home after the '69 season with normal musculature and came back looking like a bunch of Mr. Americas. We had an inordinate number of knee injuries over the next three seasons, and I believe to this day that steroids were to blame. The drugs promoted muscle growth, sure, but they did not improve the strength of connective tissues. The sheer mass of the muscles put more strain on ligaments and cartilage. It's not so difficult to figure out why the number of knee injuries made a quantum leap.

Also, the number of reported injuries throughout the league suddenly increased dramatically. In the 1960s, 75.7 percent of retired players reported physical problems that they connected to football injuries. In the '70s, that number jumped to 94.7 percent.

There was little we could do about steroids back then, however, because the league refused to take a stand. It was only after the medical profession condemned steroids, and after Steve Courson of the Pittsburgh Steelers and Lyle Alzado of the Los Angeles Raiders, among others, went public with serious health problems—negative publicity, right?—that the NFL finally acted.

It was too late for Alzado. He died of brain cancer.

By the mid-1980s, steroid use had become a league-wide problem. I would guess that, at its peak, roughly 20 percent of our players had at least experimented with steroids or growth hormones.

We did our own drug testing before the league enacted its random testing program in 1990, but our tests were not sophisticated and players found ways to beat them.

At first, it was simple. One "clean" player would carry in a good-size bottle of urine under his armpit and hide it behind the radiator in the lavatory. His buddies, who were using steroids or other drugs, just filled their bottles from the stash, which was kept warm by the radiator. We caught onto that one pretty quickly.

Other players hid a rubber container in their undershorts. When they were locked in the bathroom, they simply squeezed the rubber container to fill their bottles. Sounded just like urination, too.

Sometimes, they had their wives urinate into the rubber container.

Once, the test on a particular player came back negative, but the doctor who did the analysis was amazed to discover that the guy was pregnant. We laughed about that, but it demonstrated the lengths to which players would go to avoid detection.

By the 1990s, of course, the testing system had became more refined and it became more difficult to cheat. The league brought in its own people to monitor tests, and the players were observed as they urinated.

In a recent survey, players around the league indicated that they believed steroid use definitely was on the downturn. I would agree with that assessment.

However, a small percentage of players will always try to beat the system, and masking agents are still available. So it would be foolish to suggest that steroids have disappeared entirely from the NFL.

On the other hand, I think the league is cleaner on the whole now than at any point in the last 25 years. And that's good.

Chapter 5

Bart Starr

In 1969, the National Football League named its all-star team for the first 50 years, and John Unitas of the Baltimore Colts was selected as the quarterback.

No disrespect to Johnny U., but I don't understand how he could have been picked over Bryan Bartlett Starr.

Bart established several NFL records during his phenomenal 16-year career, perhaps the most impressive of which was a streak of 294 consecutive pass attempts without an interception (in 1964-'65). That record stood until Cleveland's Bernie Kosar broke it with 308 in 1990-'91.

Starr's career completion percentage was 57.4, at the time an NFL record. He led the league in passing three times (1962, '64 and '66), played in four Pro Bowl games, and was the Most Valuable Player in the first two Super Bowls. He threw for 23,718 yards and 152 touchdowns in his career, despite the fact that Vince Lombardi's offense was run-oriented. Starr rarely threw more than 25 passes in a game.

But, as Bart himself said, "Statistics are impressive only if they are the byproducts of winning."

Was Bart a winner? Well, he played in ten championship games and the Packers won nine of them. In those games, he completed 60.6% of his 216 pass attempts for 1,774 yards, with 15 touchdowns and three interceptions.

When the NFL's 50-year team was announced, Lombardi, who by then was coaching the Washington Redskins, was furious. He insisted that Bart, and not Unitas, should have been the quarterback.

"Bart Starr," Vince insisted, "is the greatest of all time."

It's funny, but ten years earlier, Vince could not possibly have foreseen himself making that statement. When Lombardi evaluated the Packers' quarterbacks upon his arrival in Green Bay in 1959, he saw nothing in Starr that hinted at greatness.

Starr had been selected by the Packers in the 17th round of the 1956 draft, out of Alabama. He didn't have a cannon for an arm, he was not a threat to run, and he didn't inspire fear in anybody, let alone opposing defenses.

Vince wanted his quarterback to be an extension of himself on the field—tough, demanding, fearless, a leader of men. Starr was so polite and mild-mannered, Vince didn't believe he could be a winner.

But even Vince underestimated Starr's competitiveness. Bart may not have looked or acted the part, but he had a killer instinct on the field. He also had a great work ethic and an innate feel for the game. He prepared meticulously for opponents, spending hour after hour watching film and dissecting defenses.

For the first two years, Vince played other quarterbacks. He obtained veteran Lamar McHan in a trade with the St. Louis Cardinals. When McHan got hurt, Lombardi kept Starr on the bench and sent in Joe Francis, a converted tailback. That was a real slap in the face to Bart. Later, Lombardi talked about offering "any two players on my roster" to the Dallas Cowboys for Don Meredith.

But gradually, Vince's confidence in Bart grew. The offense seemed to execute better whenever Bart was in the game, and he had leadership qualities that Vince had overlooked. Lombardi finally traded McHan early in the 1961 season and gave the job to Bart. He had earned it.

Starr turned out to be the perfect quarterback for Lombardi's system. He was a superstar without a superstar's ego. He was perfectly content handing off to Paul Hornung and Jim Taylor, and later to Elijah Pitts, Travis Williams, and Donny Anderson. He was a master at baiting defenses; nobody in the history of the game, before or since, was as effective throwing the ball off play-action fakes in third down-and-short yardage situations.

Everything Bart did, he did with a precision that Lombardi admired. And he developed a mental toughness that came back to haunt the coach at contract time.

None of the players had agents in those days; they negotiated their own contracts, and dealing with Vince, a notorious miser at contract time, was an unnerving proposition. But after the 1960 season, Bart believed he deserved a significant raise. He walked into Vince's office, and with all the courage he could muster, said, "What are we going to do about my contract?"

Vince said nothing.

"This is what I want," Bart said, naming a figure.

Vince stared at him icily, but Bart didn't back down.

"Coach, I won't settle for anything less."

Lombardi finally broke into laughter. "My God, I've created a monster!" he said. "Bart, we're not that far apart. You win."

Bart walked out of the office with a smile. But he admitted that he was wringing wet with perspiration.

A lot of pictures have been published of Bart and Vince together, both on the field and off it. People assume the two became close friends, but that wasn't the case.

They definitely had a mutual respect and a very good player-coach relationship. But Bart and Vince never socialized. Vince simply wouldn't allow himself to get close to any player, not even his starting quarterback. And I don't think Bart ever had the warm fuzzies for Lombardi; at least, not the way Jerry Kramer did. Maybe it stemmed from the way Vince treated him early in his career.

That didn't stop Bart from telling some great Lombardi jokes when he spoke at banquets.

"In a playoff game against the Los Angeles Rams, things were going so well that coach Lombardi didn't even come into the locker room at halftime," Starr said. "Instead, he bought two hot dogs and two Cokes and went out and fed 50,000 people."

Or, "Coach Lombardi had planned to be here today, but he had a little accident while he was on vacation down in Miami. He was out for a morning stroll and he was struck by a speedboat."

Bart, of course, had a squeaky clean image, and still does. And there was nothing phony about him. He was extremely polite, always saying "Please" and "Thank you," even to equipment men and ball boys. He is truly one of the finest gentlemen I have ever met.

Bart wasn't perfect, though. One day, he was in a hurry to get to Appleton for an awards banquet and nothing was going right. He yelled at his wife, Cherry, and spanked his two little boys. Cherry, fed up, finally said, "What kind of award are you going to receive, anyway?"

"A nice guy award," Bart answered sheepishly.

During his playing days, I saw him lose his temper just once. It was toward the end of his career, when he was plagued by shoulder and rib injuries.

One day, he hurt so much he was unable to finish practice. I brought him up to the training room and put him in the whirlpool. He was frustrated and angry, perhaps realizing that his playing career was coming to an end.

He slapped the sides of the whirlpool, looked at me and said, angrily, "Enough is enough." Then he lowered his head and muttered, "Who the hell do you think you are?" I'm sure he was questioning God.

The anger passed quickly. A few minutes after he got out of the whirlpool, he came back into the training room and spent 15 minutes apologizing to me. He told me he had been blessed with wonderful teammates and a fabulous career, and that football owed him nothing. He was sorry for exploding in front of me. He said it was a disgrace for him to have said the things he said.

That was Bart. Always a class act.

Unfortunately, Bart played one or two more years than he should have. He was generally one of the last players to board the team bus, and in 1970 and '71, his teammates always watched which hand he used to carry his duffle bag. If he was carrying the bag in his right hand, it was a sign that his throwing arm felt good enough for him to play. But if he was carrying his bag in his left hand, chances were good that his shoulder was bothering him and he wouldn't play that day. The players on the bus actually had contests to see who was right and who was wrong.

Unfortunately, at the end of his career, Bart carried that bag in his left hand more often than not.

I wish there was something I could have done to make those last couple of years more enjoyable for Bart. The team was going downhill, and he paid the price physically. We tried our hardest to keep him on the field, but his body was just shot.

There have been many great quarterbacks in the NFL—Unitas, Terry Bradshaw, Joe Montana, Otto Graham, Sammy Baugh, Fran Tarkenton, Sid Luckman, Dan Marino, Joe Namath . . . the list goes on and on.

I'd take Starr over all of them. In a heartbeat.

Chapter 6

Ray Nitschke

I decided to devote one chapter of this book to Bart Starr and one to Ray Nitschke because they best epitomized those great Packers teams of the 1960s. Starr and Nitschke *were* the Green Bay Packers.

Bart was unquestionably the offensive leader, and Ray his counterpart on the defensive side of the ball. In many ways, they were extensions of coach Vince Lombardi—Starr the calculating perfectionist and Nitschke the fearsome gladiator. Both got off to slow starts in their professional careers, riding the pines until Lombardi saw in them a competitive fire that he could stoke.

Although they had all those things in common, their personalities could not have been more opposite. Starr was a Southern gentleman, quiet and efficient, a pro's pro. Nitschke was a product of Chicago's mean streets, loud and tough, with an explosive temper.

Ray was one of my favorite players because of the way he approached the game. We became pretty good friends, perhaps because our backgrounds were similar. Ray was three years old when his father died and 13 when his mother passed away; I lost my father when I was 13. Ray was a skinny kid; I weighed 92 pounds as a freshman football player in high school. Ray, who grew up just outside Chicago, delivered the *Chicago Tribune* as a youth but lost his job because he broke a customer's window with a rolled-up paper; I delivered papers but lost my job because one of my customers accused me of stealing a half-pint of cream.

We both grew up poor and saw college as a way out. I didn't want to wind up working in the iron mines, 3,600 feet below the surface. Ray, who lived in the back of a tavern and was raised by an older brother, certainly wanted a better life, too.

Ray was quite a brawler as a teen. He had a rough home life, and it spilled into the streets. He got into plenty of fights and won most of them. "I felt I was somebody who didn't have anything," he said, "and I took it out on everybody."

Sports were his way out. Ray loved baseball and was a pretty good player, but he was even better on the football field. He earned a football scholarship from the University of Illinois, where he played fullback and linebacker. The Packers picked him in the third round of the 1958 draft.

Early in his career, Nitschke watched from the bench while Tom Bettis, the team's first-round draft pick in 1955, got most of the playing time at middle linebacker. Ray was frustrated because he knew he had more talent than Bettis. He tried to use humor as a salve for the pain; his favorite saying was, "I'm the judge. That's why I'm on the bench so much."

I think Lombardi saw potential in Nitschke from the beginning. But Ray was difficult to control; he was somewhat of a loose cannon, and he liked his beer. I've always believed that Vince thought he could subdue Ray, that he could reign in this wild stallion, by keeping him on the bench.

The strategy backfired. Ray grew more and more frustrated with his lack of playing time, and he became more and more obnoxious.

Once, we were in Milwaukee for a game and Ray was holed up in a bar, which was a definite no-no. Vince walked in with two friends. Now, the smartest thing Ray could have done was to get up and leave. And I mean immediately. Instead, he ordered a round of drinks for Vince and his friends.

Lombardi was livid. He turned on his heels and on the way out, he hissed at Nitschke, "You're through. You're out of here. You're history."

Vince wanted to release Ray on the spot, but the rest of the coaches talked him out of it. In order to save face with the players, Vince let them vote on it; of course, the players were unanimous in their support for Nitschke.

Eventually, Ray's fierce, take-no-prisoners approach to the game won over Lombardi. Ray and Jimmy Taylor were two players who never "brother-in-lawed it" in practice—they never went less than full throttle, and it would piss off the other players. You could never relax around Ray on the practice field—he was liable to cold-cock you with that club of a forearm he wielded.

Ray became Vince's hit man. He and Chicago's Dick Butkus became the most feared players in the NFL. I remember before the 1962 championship game, Lombardi pulled Nitschke aside and said, "Ray, remember you're the hit guy. You've got to go out there and set the pace. You've got to make people look for you. You've got to get people moving and hitting."

We had plenty of tough players on those great 1960s teams, but none tougher than Ray.

Once, we were playing in Detroit and Ray broke his arm. He came back to the defensive huddle and said, "My arm is fractured. I'm taking myself out of the game."

Dan Currie, another linebacker, said, "The hell you are. Wait until this series is over."

With only one arm, Ray managed to get in two good licks. One of them was so good, in fact, that he broke his nose. That's right: A broken arm and a broken nose on the same series. The game ended in a 13-13 tie, and Ray was more angry about the score than he was his condition.

Another time, the Lions were kicking our butts. Ray came off the field and I said, "Boy, Detroit is playing good and hard. They're up emotionally and we seem to be down."

Ray exploded. He got in my face. "What the hell do you mean, we're down?" he said. "You should never be down in a football game. Never!"

And Ray never was.

The most amazing thing about Nitschke is that he played his entire career on one leg. His left leg had been injured so often in high school and college, the muscles had atrophied and they never fully regenerated. His left leg was 50 percent smaller in circumference than his right. I'm not sure if anybody but Bud Jorgensen and I knew about it. He never said a word, never complained. But I can tell you his left knee was very heavily taped throughout his 15-year career.

In 1972, Ray tore his right hamstring prior to another game against the Lions. The back of his leg, from his groin to his knee, was black— the result of hemorrhaged muscle tissue. He played against Detroit on Sunday, and if my math is correct, he played on only one-half of one leg.

Ray had great study habits and analyzed as much film as Starr. He used to drive Lombardi crazy during practice because he was able to call out almost all of the offensive plays just before the snap. He would run around screaming, "Watch out for the pass; watch out for the draw!" Vince would tell him to shut up. Ray would just grin; after a play or two, he would start screaming again.

Deep down, I think Vince enjoyed this ritual. If Nitschke could figure out the plays, then opposing scouts up in the press box probably could, too. It made the offense work harder to disguise the plays.

Ray was one of the few players who wasn't intimidated by Vince. He didn't really settle down off the field until he married Jackie. A stable family life probably was the best thing that ever happened to him.

Nitschke struggled, emotionally and physically, toward the end of his career. His legs were shot, but he still thought he could play. He didn't want to give it up.

He was a bitter, frustrated man as he stood on the sideline at Milwaukee County Stadium on Nov. 5, 1972, watching his beloved Packers defeat the San Francisco 49ers. Lombardi had died two years earlier. Starr was still calling the plays, but as an assistant coach. Most of Nitschke's teammates from the championship seasons had retired.

Coach Dan Devine had replaced Nitschke in the starting lineup with a young Jim Carter, and as the weeks went by in '72, Nitschke sensed that the end was near for him, too.

Now, in the final minutes of a 34-24 victory over the 49ers, Devine was motioning for Nitschke to go into the game for Carter.

Mop-up duty, for arguably the greatest middle linebacker who ever played the game?

Nitschke's pride was stung.

"I told him, 'No, I'm not going in there,'" Nitschke recounted. "I was really mad, frustrated. It was a pride thing."

Nitschke walked away from Devine. Then he started thinking it over. He looked into the sea of faces at County Stadium, many of them familiar.

He owed it to them.

One last goodbye.

"As mad as I was at Devine, I thought about my career and, man, I had to go in there," Nitschke said. "So I go in the game, but I'm really angry. I'm mad as hell, right? There's a timeout, and they announce my name: 'Ray Nitschke is now playing middle linebacker.'

"There was a tremendous ovation. And in one instant, I went from hate to tremendous love for those Packer fans. It was unbelievable how I felt at that moment. I had tears streaming down my face. It was truly one of the great moments of my career.

"That made me so proud to be a Packer."

Ray was voted the greatest middle linebacker of the NFL's first 50 years. He was inducted into the Pro Football Hall of Fame in 1978, one year after Starr gained admittance.

A lot of people have taken Ray for granted over the years because he has been so accessible. Perhaps because of his background, he has great empathy for people, especially children. He has always been available for speaking engagements and charity functions. In that way, he has been a tremendous ambassador for the Green Bay Packers and for the NFL.

Plenty of great linebackers have come and gone, but there will never be another quite like Ray Nitschke.

Chapter 7

Players I Have Known

Over the years, I saw literally thousands of players come and go in Green Bay. A few were extraordinarily talented and made the Hall of Fame. Others contributed to the rich history of the Packers in less spectacular fashion. And many more were in Green Bay for just a few days, or a few games—players whose names and faces I barely remember.

You can't meet as many players as I have met without coming across a few characters and the occasional renegade. You can't tape as many ankles as I have taped without hearing some great stories.

Here are a few of my favorites—the players, and their stories.

LIONEL ALDRIDGE (DE, 1963-'71)

I'll never forget Lionel's first pre-season game. He was so nervous and pumped up that he was hyperventilating, so he took himself out of the game.

He came over and kneeled beside me on the sideline, and I assumed there had been a substitution.

Suddenly, Vince Lombardi whirled and came stomping over.

"Aldridge, what are you doing?" Lombardi barked.

Lionel just looked up and said, "I came out of the game, coach."

Well, Lombardi got in Lionel's face and went into one of his patented tirades, the kind that made the veins in his neck stand out, the kind that made you wish you were somewhere—anywhere—else.

"You don't come out of a game!" he screamed. "You stay in a game until you're taken out. Don't ever do that again."

Lionel became a very good player and an outstanding big-game performer. Some guys disappear in pressure situations. Not Lionel. He had a huge heart, and he loved to play for Lombardi. He was one of those guys who would do anything for the man.

And tough? Lionel broke a bone in his lower leg during an exhibition game one year and it looked as though he would miss six weeks. He stayed in the cast for two weeks, had it taken off, and played a week later. Lombardi encouraged him, saying, "That bone is not a weight-bearing bone."

Unfortunately, Lionel developed some personal problems near the end of his career, when he was playing for the San Diego Chargers. It didn't help that many of his teammates there were involved in one of the worst drug scandals the NFL has ever seen.

He came back to Wisconsin after his playing career ended, and for a while he did very well. He worked full-time at WTMJ in Milwaukee, doing both TV and radio. NBC Sports spotted his local sportscasts and asked him to work on the network's regular-season NFL games. In January 1977, he was an analyst for Super Bowl XI.

But nobody knew then that Lionel was mentally ill. He had been hallucinating since 1974. He saw people who weren't there and heard words that weren't spoken. For a while, he was able to fight the demons and function, but by late 1977 the hallucinations had become terrifying. He was paranoid that people were trying to hurt him. He heard imaginary gunshots and fell to the ground.

Finally, Lionel was committed to the Milwaukee County Mental Health Complex. He was diagnosed as a paranoid schizophrenic. He accepted therapy but rejected the medication that could have helped him.

"I can lick this thing by myself," he said.

He was wrong. His world collapsed. His wife sued for divorce. He lost his job. And for the next seven years, Aldridge lived a nightmare existence—mentally ill, sometimes seeking treatment, sometimes walking away from it. He drifted in and out of reality and in and out of society. He lived briefly in a college dorm at Utah State, his alma mater. One night in Salt Lake City, he took off his Super Bowl ring, the one with three diamonds signifying the Packers' three NFL championships, placed it in his pocket, and fell asleep on the sidewalk. When he woke up, the ring was gone.

Lionel showed up at our training camp to watch workouts one year, and he was shoeless and shirtless. I went up to him and said, "Lionel, that's a bit out of character for you, isn't it?" He had always been an impeccable dresser.

He just kind of stared at me and didn't say anything. Later that day, I saw him eating lunch with the team and said hello, and got another blank stare in return. I was really frightened for him at that point.

Lionel wandered back to Milwaukee and checked into a rescue mission. His paranoia worsened. Finally, he checked into the Milwaukee County Mental Health Complex again. Doctors told him that a powerful drug, Haldol, could control the chemical imbalance in his brain. Lionel hated the medicine's side effects—impotence, a protruding tongue, stiffening of the limbs—but he made a commitment to Haldol and his condition improved.

The hallucinations went away and eventually he had the dosage reduced from 35 milligrams daily to just one milligram daily.

After two years of treatment and therapy, Lionel took a job in the post office in Milwaukee. The last time I saw him was at Ron

Kostelnik's funeral in early 1993. He seemed healthy and content with his life.

After all Lionel has been through, he deserves that much.

DONNY ANDERSON (RB, 1966-'71)

Donny was one of the first players to benefit from the bidding war between the American Football League and the NFL. He was a bonus baby, one of the "Gold Dust Twins," along with fullback Jim Grabowski.

But if he thought he was going to get special treatment from Vince Lombardi, he found out in a hurry that that wasn't the case. If anything, Lombardi bent over backward to give him a hard time during his rookie season.

He had come to training camp trying to shake the effects of a sprained ankle that he had suffered getting ready for the College All-Star Game. He thought he was going to be able to rest the ankle a little when he reported, but Lombardi made him suit up and practice.

On the first day of camp, he twisted the ankle and fell to the turf, writhing in pain. Bud Jorgensen and I started to run onto the field and Lombardi yelled, "Leave him alone. Let him crawl off, if he has to. There are no gimpers on this team."

I think Donny learned right there what to expect in the NFL. Especially Vince's NFL.

Donny learned another lesson in the second game of the season, this time from veteran guard Fuzzy Thurston. We trailed the Cleveland Browns, 20-14, with less than two minutes to play, and they had the ball. Donny turned to Fuzzy and said, "Well, it looks like we're going to lose this one."

Fuzzy looked at him disdainfully and said, "Kid, here's what's going to happen. The defense will hold them, we'll get the ball and drive down for a touchdown, kick the extra point and beat them, 21-20. Then we'll get on the plane and go home."

Of course, that's exactly what happened. Jim Taylor scored with seven seconds left to tie the score and Don Chandler kicked the decisive point.

Donny played sparingly in the first half of his rookie year, because Vince didn't believe in playing rookies. He thought the only thing they were good for was special teams. But in Game Seven, Donny scored two touchdowns in a 56-3 blowout of the Atlanta Falcons, one of them on a 77-yard punt return.

Lombardi told him, "I think you've found a job."

Anderson broke into the starting lineup in '67 and scored four touchdowns in his first start, a 55-7 crunching of the Browns. He led the Packers in rushing from 1968 through '70 and played in the 1969 Pro Bowl.

One of Donny's jobs was holding for extra points and field goals. One year, we had an eccentric kicker who complained about Donny's holds whenever he missed. The kicker would come to the sideline and tell Grabowski that the ball wasn't tilted at the right angle or that the laces weren't in the proper position.

Well, Grabowski finally told Anderson what was going on. On the first snap the next day at practice, Donny caught the ball, whirled and threw it at the kicker's feet. "Get your own damn holder," he said, and walked off the field.

In 1970, Donny was the NFL's fourth-leading rusher with 853 yards. He played one more season for the Packers before Dan Devine traded him to the St. Louis Cardinals for running back MacArthur Lane. Packers fans thought it was a bad trade, but it turned out to be a good change of scenery for both players. Donny had become unhappy in Green Bay, and Lane was disgruntled in St. Louis.

In 1972, Lane played an important role as the lead blocker for John Brockington, who carried us to the Central Division title. Donny played three seasons for the Cardinals before retiring.

KEN BOWMAN (C, 1964-'73)

Kenny played center for the Packers for ten years, and the last five seasons, he played in tremendous pain.

Ken suffered dislocations of both shoulders early in his career, and the injuries bothered him the rest of his playing days.

Every Monday during the season, Ken came into the training room for therapy. Many times, he could not lift his arms above his chest. He would soak in the whirlpool for a while, just to try to loosen them up. Then we would slowly and painstakingly begin to work on increasing his range of motion.

We gave Ken ultrasound treatments, but diathermy was out—he had one of his AC joints wired down and we were concerned that deep heat would cause bone problems.

Kenny was the kind of guy who could play in pain, which Lombardi, of course, admired. Once, just a couple of days after one of his dislocations, he came into the locker room and demanded to be taped. Then he went out and hit the seven-man sled, as if nothing had happened. It was unbelievable. I think even Lombardi was surprised.

JOHN BROCKINGTON (RB, 1971-'77)

John, a vicious runner from Ohio State, was the first running back in NFL history to rush for 1,000 yards in each of his first three seasons. Not only was he a devastating runner with pistons for legs, but he was a great guy. And he loved to play football.

In 1971, John's rookie year, we were playing the Cincinnati Bengals in Green Bay. John burst through a hole on one play and Ken Dyer, the Bengals' safety, came up to meet him. Dyer tried to get low to take out John's churning legs. Unfortunately, he dropped his head and one of John's knees caught him flush on the helmet. It was very similar to the collision between Nelson Toburen and Johnny Unitas that ended Toburen's career ten years earlier.

Dyer wasn't as lucky as Toburen, however. He was temporarily paralyzed from the neck down. He spent about five weeks at St. Mary's Hospital in Green Bay before he began to regain some movement.

Dyer's football career was over, obviously, and he moved to Phoenix. A couple of years later, we went there for a mini-camp, and he came over to watch us practice. It was amazing how much his condition had improved. He was able to drive a car and stand erect, and he walked with only a slight shuffle.

John was so bothered by the incident, however, that I wonder to this day if it didn't contribute to his mysterious collapse. He averaged 5.1 yards per carry in 1971, but his average dipped to 3.7 the next year. After his third season, his production fell off dramatically, and in his sixth and last full season with the Packers, he was just a shell of his former self; hesitant and indecisive with the ball, he often seemed to be running in place.

Despite playing only six seasons (plus one game) with the Packers, John still ranks number two on the team's career rushing list with 5,024 yards.

BOB BROWN (DT, 1966-'73)

What a great athlete. Whenever we needed a big defensive play, it seemed like Bob was the one who made something happen. He was as responsible for our championship seasons in the mid-'60s as any player on the roster.

Bob was never into conditioning or weight lifting. He felt he had God-given strength, and that was all he needed. And he was one rough, tough son of a gun.

Once, he took himself out of a game in Minnesota and came over to me on the sideline. "Domenic, check my leg," he said. "I have a little bit of a knot in there or something."

I examined his leg, but couldn't find anything wrong.

"No problem," he said. "Don't worry about it. We'll get by somehow."

He went back in and played the rest of the game. The next morning, his leg was swollen, so we sent him to get some X-rays. Sure enough, it was broken. He had played the entire game against the Vikings on a broken leg.

I'll give you another example of Bob's toughness. He was driving home from a card game one night during the off-season, and one of his passengers had lost big money. He and Bob started to argue, and the guy pulled out a .22 revolver and shot Bob in the neck. Bob calmly drove himself to the hospital and had the wound dressed.

The next year at training camp, I told him, "We're going to make a sign for your helmet. It's going to say, 'How do you expect to stop me when a bullet couldn't?'"

He got a kick out of that one.

Bob also was a great cook. He loved cooking exotic dishes and wild game. One of his favorites was raccoon. One day, while he was at practice, his car was stolen. The police finally tracked it down in Upper Michigan.

"We found it," one of the policeman told Bob, "but geez, Bob, there were two 'coons in the car."

Without missing a beat, Bob, who is black, said, "Of course there were 'coons in the car. What did you expect?"

We both laughed so hard, we nearly fell to the ground.

CARLOS BROWN (QB, 1975-'76)

Actor Alan Autry plays Carroll O'Connor's handsome, no-nonsense sidekick, "Bubba Skinner," on the popular television drama, "In the Heat of the Night."

In another life, Autry was Carlos Brown, reserve quarterback for the Green Bay Packers.

Carlos has had numerous other roles in film and TV shows since he hung up his spikes. He has appeared in the movies "Amazing Grace and Chuck" with Gregory Peck, "Southern Comfort" with Keith Carradine, "North Dallas Forty" with Nick Nolte, and "Popeye" with Robin Williams. He also has landed guest appearances on the TV shows "Cheers," "Newhart," and "St. Elsewhere." He was cast in the NBC miniseries "The Great Los Angeles Earthquake," and his TV movies include "Countdown," "Street of Dreams," and "Proud Men."

One of the themes of "In the Heat of the Night" is black-white relationships. Carlos comes from a poor background. His family didn't even have a telephone until he went away to college on a football scholarship.

"I get mad when I hear blacks say, 'You don't understand,' " Carlos once said. "I can relate to a poor black man better than I can to a rich white man."

Carlos lives in Northern California and remains a loyal Packer backer. "Once a Packer, always a Packer," he said. "I'm really behind coach [Mike] Holmgren."

Brown's shot as a professional quarterback came late in the 1976 season, after starter Lynn Dickey was injured. Brown, a 12th-round draft choice in '75, started three games, but completed just 26 of 74 attempts for 333 yards, with 2 touchdowns and 6 interceptions. Green Bay lost all three games.

Coach Bart Starr had seen enough. He summoned Brown to his office to inform him that he was being relieved of his starting job. Starr liked Brown personally and complimented him on his work ethic, but Brown was upset.

"I said something like, 'I'll come back to haunt you,' " Brown said. "I didn't know at that time that it would be on the TV screen."

Looking back on his brief stay in Green Bay, Brown realizes now that he wasn't talented enough to play quarterback in the NFL. He had played the position for only two years at the University of Pacific; he was injured his junior year, and was moved to tight end his senior year. If he came out of college today with that kind of background, he wouldn't even be drafted.

But Carlos made a lasting impression on me. He always called me "Domo," and the nickname stuck. I would bet that, over the years, I've been called "Domo" more than one million times by players, coaches and friends.

ROBERT BROWN (DE, 1982-'92)

Robert came out of Virginia Tech as a 240-pound linebacker, and although the coaches were impressed with his work habits and his conditioning, they knew, early on, that he wasn't going to make the team as a linebacker.

I was in a personnel meeting with coach Starr and some of the position coaches, and they were agonizing over having to cut Robert.

I listened for a while, then I raised my hand and said, "How much weight do you think Robert could put on?" The coaches looked at each other and one of them said, "I think, with his frame, he could get up to 260 or 270, maybe even 280."

"Well, why don't you try him at defensive end?" I asked.

The room got kind of quiet. Evidently, when I left, the coaches decided to give my suggestion a shot. I was happy for Robert because he is such a great gentleman.

He went on to be a productive player for a decade, never a star but always reliable and consistent.

In 1992, after the last home game of the season—my final game in Lambeau Field and, as it turned out, Robert's, too—we walked off the field and Robert put his arm around me and we both had a pretty good cry.

LEROY BUTLER (CB-S, 1990-)

Early in the 1992 season, shortly after I had announced my decision to retire, LeRoy sauntered into the training room and said, "I really like you, Domo, and I appreciate the job you do. I'd like to buy you something as a token of my appreciation. Do you like Rolex watches?"

I thought he was putting me on, or that maybe I was going to be the target of some sort of prank.

So, naturally, I went along with it.

"Heck, yeah, LeRoy, I'd love to have a Rolex," I said.

He laughed and I chuckled a little bit, and he walked out of the room. As the season went on, I forget about our conversation. Then, one day I picked up the *Green Bay Press-Gazette,* and there was a story about my upcoming retirement. The story quoted LeRoy, and he told the reporter that he was going to buy me a Rolex.

When LeRoy came in the next day, I said, "LeRoy, are you out of your mind? You know you're not going to buy me a Rolex watch. Why would you put something like that in the paper?"

He just shook his head and laughed. About two days later, he came into the training room, hopped up onto the table to get taped and said, "Do you want diamonds on that Rolex, or not?"

I thought he was going too far, but I said, "Well, LeRoy, I'm going to leave that up to you, but I'd just as soon not have diamonds, because those things look a little bit out of my class."

On the final day of the season, LeRoy came in with a box. I knew this had to be the final joke: I would tear open the box and something would jump out of it.

I opened the box slowly, and inside was the most beautiful watch I had ever seen. I couldn't believe it.

That Rolex means as much to me as any award or honor I have ever received, because it came not from an organization or club, but from one of the players. And it came from the heart.

Thank you, LeRoy.

RICH CAMPBELL (QB, 1981-'84)

Rich was drafted in the first round out of the University of California in 1981. He was big, intelligent, and had pretty good speed for a guy his size and a strong enough arm. But he played very little in the four years he was with the Packers, and I still can't figure out why he didn't pan out.

I was not able to get onto the practice field the first time he threw, during a minicamp shortly after the draft, but I was anxious to find out how he fared.

After practice, I stopped Zeke Bratkowski and said, "Well, how'd the new man look?"

Zeke just said, "Well, it was kind of windy out there."

I got a very sick feeling in my stomach.

Campbell had put up great numbers at California, but if he lacked anything, it was intensity. He expressed an interest in becoming a minister after his career was over, and I sometimes wondered if he had the killer instinct that every professional football player must have.

Whatever chance Rich had to make it was destroyed by some of the coaches. They really got down on him, particularly offensive coordinator Bob Schnelker, who openly talked to the media about Rich's limitations. It got to the point where the team president, Judge Robert J. Parins, intervened and told the coaches to stop criticizing Rich publicly.

Rich did have one shining moment, a desperation pass to Phil Epps with seconds left that beat the Chicago Bears at Soldier Field.

Rich eventually did become a minister and is very happy today.

As a player, though, he sure was an enigma.

FRED CARR (LB, 1968-'77)

During Freddie's rookie year, he lost a game ticket for his wife, and he approached Vince Lombardi—who was then the general manager—and asked for a replacement.

Vince chewed him up and down.

"Don't you ever, ever come to me and tell me you lost a ticket for your wife," Lombardi scolded him. "Your wife is a very important part of this business, a very important part of this football team, and you'd better take care of her."

Freddie could hardly believe what he was hearing. Here was the general manager of a pro football team, giving him a sermon on his relationship with his wife! It floored him.

Freddie was a tremendous athlete—big, strong, and cat-quick. He used his speed to disrupt offenses and blow up plays. A linebacker would come along years later and remind me of the way Carr played. His name is Lawrence Taylor.

Unfortunately, Freddie's supporting cast on defense was pretty dismal throughout his career, and he performed in relative obscurity. Still, he played in the Pro Bowl twice, a testimony to the respect he had earned throughout the league.

Freddie seemed to love playing football, but late in his career he changed. He was making somewhere around $80,000, which in those days was pretty good money, but he suddenly and inexplicably lost his zest for the game.

I ran into him one day in the parking lot and he said, "Dom, I think I've had it."

I said, "Freddie, what are you talking about?"

He said, "Ahhh, my knee is bothering me. I'm done."

He had a cyst on his knee that needed draining, but it certainly was not a career-threatening condition.

"Freddie, there's nothing wrong with that knee that can't be rehabbed after minor surgery," I told him.

He just waved me off and walked away. Even Alden Roche, his best friend on the team, didn't know what had gotten into him.

Carr wound up contacting an attorney, who made a big fuss about the knee. Eventually, Freddie and the Packers settled for $10,000.

It made me sick that Freddie did that. It was just a very poor decision. He probably could have played five more years and commanded an annual salary of $120,000 or more.

I don't know. Maybe he just got tired of losing.

DON CHANDLER (K, 1965-'67)

Don came to Green Bay from the New York Giants in a trade in 1965, and the move thrilled him because he was not a big-city guy.

When it became evident that he was going to be traded, he persuaded the Giants to send him to the Packers instead of the Dallas Cowboys because he wanted to join the team that had beaten the Giants' brains out in the 1961 and '62 NFL championship games.

Don was one of the last kicking specialists to handle both place-kicking and punting duties, and he did both jobs very well. In his first year in Green Bay, he averaged 42.9 yards per punt, including a Packers record 90-yarder. He finished fifth in the NFL in punting, and also made 17 of 26 field goals (65.3%), a very good percentage then.

He will forever be remembered for the controversial field goal that beat the Baltimore Colts in the 1965 Western Conference championship game. To this day, Don Shula, then the Colts coach and now the coach of the Miami Dolphins, insists that his team was robbed. Chandler's kick sailed high above the upright and appeared to drift wide. Even Chandler turned away in disgust, thinking he had missed.

But Bart Starr, who was the holder, watched it all the way and said the ball went through the upright and then curved out. If that's what Bart says, then it's so. He's the most honest man I know. At any rate, the kick was so controversial, the NFL raised the height of the uprights the next year.

That field goal was very important to the Packers, who went on to win NFL titles in 1965, '66, and '67 and the first two Super Bowls. Had Donny missed, who knows if we would have won any of them?

Don had a superb game in Super Bowl II. He was 33 years old at the time and made four field goals from 20, 31, 39, and 43 yards; he also kicked three extra points for a total of 15 points.

Despite playing only three seasons for the Packers, Chandler ranks 15th on the Packers' all-time scoring list with 261 points.

PAUL COFFMAN (TE, 1978-'85)

In 1978, some of the coaches wanted to sign a rough, tough free-agent tight end named Paul Coffman. They were a little skeptical that he could play, however, because he had lost 45 percent of his range of motion in both elbows. The team doctors were concerned that he would be seriously injured.

My argument for signing him was that he had had the condition since he was 12 years old. He played football in grade school, high school and college and didn't have any problem with his elbows.

Domenic Gentile, Head Trainer, Green Bay Packers

Domenic (front row, seated, sixth from left) at St. Mary's School, Hurley, Wisconsin, 1943

Hurley High School, 1947 state basketball runnersup. Gentile is seated, front row at right.

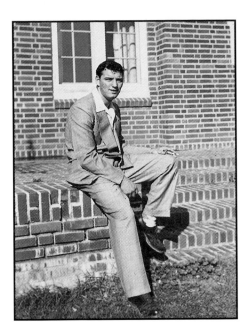

A senior at North Dakota State, 1951.

Right: An ambidextrous basketball star at North Dakota State. *Below:* Dom (third from left) with army buddies in 1952.

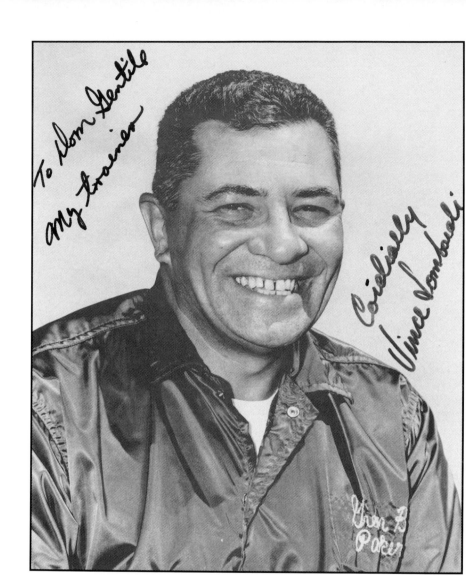

"You're my trainer!"

"Dom was far more than just the team trainer. He was one of us."
(Photo: Vernon J. Biever)

Miles and miles of Packer tape.

President Ford visits the Packer training room. (No. 81 is Rich McGeorge.) (Photos on this page by Vernon J. Biever)

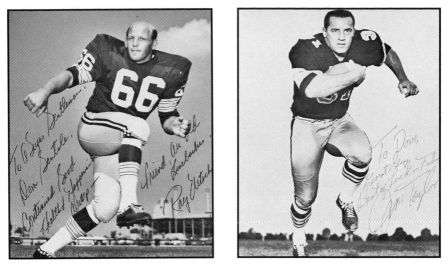

Two of the greatest—Nitschke and Taylor.

Packers, including Bart Starr and Paul Hornung (center left and right) at Vince Lombardi's funeral. (Photo: Vernon J. Biever)

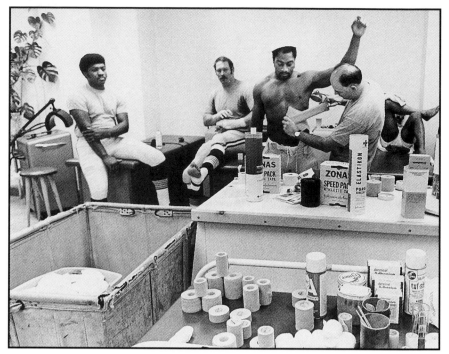

Taping up MacArthur Lane.
(Photo: Vernon J. Biever)

Injuries—inevitable part of the game.
(Photo: David Garot)

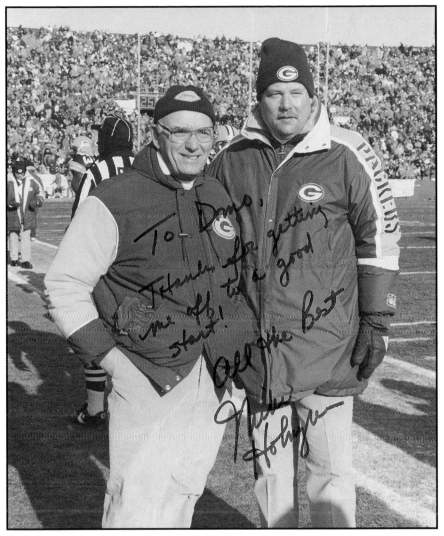

Dom with Coach Mike Holmgren.
(Photo: Vernon J. Biever)

With equipment manager Bob Noel (l) and Paul Hornung.

Domenic with family at last game as Packer trainer.
(Photo: Vernon J. Biever)

Time running down.
(Photo: David Garot)

A lifetime of memories.

Somebody must have listened to me, because we did sign Paul. He became the most productive tight end in Packers history, catching 322 passes—sixth on the team's all-time list—for 4,223 yards and 39 touchdowns.

I always admired Paul because he got the most out of his limited talent. He wasn't very big and he certainly wasn't fast. He made plays through hard work and determination.

Once, in a game against the Dallas Cowboys, Coffman caught a pass over the middle. Everson Walls, a very good cornerback, came in low to make the tackle and Paul just hurdled him and picked up 15 more yards. It was the kind of play that Coffman never could have made in practice. When you put the ball in his hands in a game, though, he responded.

TOMMY JOE CRUTCHER (LB, 1964-'67, '71-'72)

Tommy Joe wasn't a superstar on those great Packers teams of the 1960s, but he was a good, smart, dependable player. He was a Texan through and through, the sort of guy you pictured sitting on a horse in the middle of nowhere. And in fact, after he got out of football he went back to Texas and bought a 24,000-acre ranch.

Once, Tommy got his bell rung during a game in Milwaukee. We got him off the field and he was pretty disoriented, so I gave him the scoreboard test. Some trainers ask players to count backward from 10, or ask them what city they're playing in; I always had the players try to read the scoreboard.

"Tommy, can you read the fan-a-gram?" I asked him.

He said, "Oh yeah, fan-a-gram, fan-a-gram, fan-a-gram . . . oh boy, fan-a-gram, fan-a-gram, fan-a-gram."

Needless to say, we sat Tommy down for the rest of the game.

Tommy distinguished himself on the football field, but he was even better at another game. He was the best poker player on our team, if not the best in the whole league. Tommy once told me—and other players verified his story—that for two years, he did not cash a single paycheck from the Packers. He lived off his prolific poker winnings.

Unlike Paul Hornung, Tommy didn't have a reputation as being a ladies' man, but in his own quiet way he had a knack for attracting female companionship. Women liked his company, his sense of humor, and perhaps some other things.

Tommy was at a bar one night and when he was ready to leave, a couple of women volunteered to go with him. They were married, but that didn't seem to bother Tommy. A third woman also expressed an interest in joining them. Tommy didn't argue, of course.

When he woke up the next morning, the three women were gone and so was his Super Bowl ring. He called the two married women and both of them told him the third woman had taken the ring. But he couldn't file a report with the police, because then the names of the married women would have been made public.

Tommy simply contacted the company that had made the rings and ordered a duplicate.

A few years later, a man found Tommy's original ring on the floor of a bar. The man contacted a newspaper reporter, who called Tommy. The reporter asked if Tommy wanted to buy back the original.

"How much is he asking?" Crutcher asked.

"The guy wants $18,000," the reporter said.

Crutcher laughed.

"Hell, I'm nostalgic, but I ain't $18,000 worth of nostalgic. Tell him good luck trying to sell it."

CARROLL DALE (WR, 1965-'72)

Carroll, Tom Brown, and I always sat together on the team plane and played cribbage. Once in a while, we'd go crazy and start playing for 50 cents a hand, or even a dollar.

Once, I got on a roll while we were playing double or nothing. I kept winning and saying, "Come on, double or nothing, double or nothing." After several hands, Carroll and Tom each owed me $300.

They got very quiet. I could have quit right there, collected $600—and probably lost two good friends. So I kept playing until I lost. Finally, Tom and Carroll could laugh again.

Carroll was one of my favorite players and people. He was polite, easy to get along with—and one hell of a wide receiver.

He came to us from the Los Angeles Rams in a trade, and after the Packers cut him in 1972 he spent one more season with the Minnesota Vikings before retiring. He finished his career with 439 receptions for 8,271 yards and 52 touchdowns, and he played in three Pro Bowl games.

Dale's most memorable catch with the Packers was in the 1965 NFL championship game. He went into the huddle and told Bart Starr to throw it long, because the defensive back was playing him tight.

Carroll ran straight up the field on a fly pattern. Bart underthrew the ball a little, but Carroll adjusted, came back for the ball and then turned the defender around with a great fake. It was one of those plays where, as you watch it develop, you have absolutely no doubt that it is going to go for a touchdown.

Carroll didn't have great speed but he ran precise routes and had great hip and shoulder fakes. He always seemed to be able to get past defenders.

He told me recently that the talent level at wide receiver today is extremely high, but he lamented that the art of putting a move on a defender has disappeared in recent years because receivers rely almost solely on their speed. He said that if the receivers combined moves with their raw speed, many of them would be almost unstoppable.

LYNN DICKEY (QB, 1976-'85)

In 1971, Lynn was drafted number three by the Houston Oilers. As a rookie in Houston, he dislocated and broke his left hip, which put him out for a year and severely hampered him for the rest of his career.

It seemed that all of Lynn's injuries after he came to Green Bay—and there were many—occurred on his left side. His left ankle was weak; he fractured both the tibia and fibula in his left leg; he had chronic soreness in his left foot. I'm convinced that his problems stemmed from that hip injury.

Many people questioned our judgment to let Lynn continue to play later in his career, when he was held together by tape, braces, flak jackets, and special pads. And, in fact, I know the coaches hinted at retirement several times, but Lynn wouldn't even consider it.

He had been drafted in 1971, the year of the quarterback. Archie Manning, Dan Pastorini, Jim Plunkett, and Kenny Anderson also were drafted that year. Lynn really believed that he was as good as any of those quarterbacks, and he spent his entire career trying to prove it. He was always looking for that big moment, that big game, that big season. Unfortunately, he had very few of those in Green Bay.

Lynn really enjoyed the 1982 season, even though it was shortened by the players strike. We went 5-3-1 and made the playoffs, and Lynn's ego was fed somewhat by our modest success.

Lynn was a fine pocket passer with a rifle arm and a great feel for the game. He had some fantastic performances for us, because, despite all of his physical limitations, he could really throw the football.

He put on an unforgettable passing clinic in a blizzard at Mile High Stadium during a Monday night game against the Denver Broncos in 1984. We lost, 17-14, but Dickey was incredible. He was the only player, it seemed, who managed to stay on his feet for most of the plays, and he threw with pinpoint accuracy. One of the headlines in a Denver newspaper the next day read "Dickey A Wizard In The Blizzard." His counterpart with the Broncos, John Elway, struggled all night, and some of his teammates later told our players that he was awe-struck watching Lynn throw the ball.

But Lynn's injuries had severely limited his mobility, and he took a lot of vicious shots over the years. He was extremely tough. Most people wouldn't go to a tea party with some of the injuries he had, and he was out there getting nailed by blitzing linebackers.

I'll never forget the 1983 season opener against the Houston Oilers in the Astrodome. Lynn had been suffering with a bad back and had taken an epidural injection. But the needle had penetrated too far and gone into his spinal column, and he was suffering from pounding headaches.

Whenever the defense was on the field, Lynn lay on the turf with his feet up on the bench in order to get some relief. Then, when we'd get the ball, he'd strap on his helmet and proceed to shred the Oilers' secondary with pinpoint passes. We won the game, 41-38.

I watched Lynn play with a fractured coccyx (imagine what it felt like when he was thrown to the turf on the seat of his pants). I watched him play with three fractured vertebra in his lower back—not a debilitating injury, but one that certainly had to be very painful.

Throughout Lynn's tenure as the Packers' starting quarterback, we had, for the most part, a porous offensive line. It seemed that Lynn was always running—or, more accurately, limping—for his life.

One year, he wore braces on both knees. Some people thought that was odd, since his knees were among the few body parts that he had not broken, torn or somehow damaged. I think Lynn wore them as an insurance policy because he knew he could not escape a pass rush and he wanted to protect himself as much as possible.

Lynn had a great football mind. Sometimes, he questioned the game plan or some aspects of the offense, which got him into hot water with the coaches. He was pretty adamant, pretty sure of himself that way.

I always thought he would have made a fine coach, but coaching never appealed to him. He had neither the patience nor the inclination. If Lynn couldn't be out there zinging bullets to James Lofton or John Jefferson, he wanted no part of the game.

BRETT FAVRE (QB, 1992-)

The more I'm around Brett, the more I see Bart Starr, Fran Tarkenton, and Johnny Unitas.

Brett's got a fire in the pit of his stomach. He's as tough as they come. He makes mistakes, sure, but he also makes plays, and that's the mark of a great quarterback.

Even though I'm retired, it's going to be fun to watch Brett as he continues to develop under coach Mike Holmgren. I don't think he's a fly-by-nighter. I think he's going to be the Packers' quarterback—and a good one—for many years.

Brett developed a reputation as a reckless, fun-loving party animal during his rookie year with the Atlanta Falcons in 1991. He was young, he wasn't playing, and, by his own admission, he wasn't mature. He was known for his willingness to visit a nightclub or two in the early morning hours.

But Brett is no fool. When Packers general manager Ron Wolf obtained him in an off-season trade in February, 1992, he recognized the opportunity and got serious about his football career.

Unfortunately, his reputation preceded him.

Brett likes to tell the story about his first visit to Green Bay, shortly after the trade. He and his agent, James "Bus" Cook, arrived at Austin Straubel airport and caught a cab.

Cook wanted to test the local reaction to the trade for Atlanta's third-string quarterback, so he struck up a conversation with the cabbie.

"I hear the Packers have a new quarterback," Cook said.

"Yeah, the guy's name is Tricia something," the cabbie said.

"Isn't his name Favre?" Cook asked.

"No, it's Trish, and he's a troublemaker," the cabbie responded. "He's already been kicked out of three bars here for fighting."

Favre, of course, had been in Green Bay for all of 20 minutes.

A few months later, Favre and safety Tim Hauck hailed a cab, and Brett instantly recognized the cabbie as the Favre-basher. The cabbie still didn't recognize him.

This time, Hauck decided to have a little fun.

"Aren't those Packers a bunch of so-and-sos?" Hauck said.

"Yeah, you ain't kidding," the cabbie said.

"Especially that quarterback, Favre," Hauck added.

"Yeah, we've had problems with him ever since he came to town," the cabbie said. "The Packers can't keep the guy out of trouble."

Favre has had a hard time shaking that image. Some people still perceive him to be an undisciplined, unsophisticated kid from Kiln, Mississippi, who is more interested in having a good time than winning football games for the Packers.

I see just the opposite. My impression of Brett is that he is an intelligent young man who is all business when it comes to football. He's a very likable guy. He has natural leadership skills; he goes out of his way to encourage teammates, and I think they believe in him.

Brett is only going to get better and better. Just watch. In my opinion, acquiring Brett Favre was the Packers' most important personnel move in at least a decade.

ANGELO FIELDS (T, 1982)

Angelo had a ton of talent, but there was just one problem: He also weighed a ton.

When he came to us in a trade with the Houston Oilers, he was grossly overweight; he tipped the scales at about 360 pounds.

Fields had a funny line about his battle of the bulge. He described himself as a light eater. "As soon as it gets light," he said, "I start to eat."

The Oilers picked him in the second round of the 1980 draft, but they gave up on him after two seasons. Our coaches saw him as a project. They were determined to turn him back into a player, so they sent him to the "fat farm" at Duke University. He stuck to the program and lost a lot of weight; when he came back to Green Bay, he weighed 289.

The coaches kept an eye on him, and he stuck to his weight maintenance program. He was looking pretty good. Then, he asked for permission to leave Green Bay for a weekend to visit friends in East Lansing, Mich., where he had been a star at Michigan State. The coaches let him go.

He came back three days later, and his weight had ballooned to 320. That's right, he had somehow managed to gain 30 pounds in three days. I don't know how many calories he consumed in those 72 hours, but it must have been enough to fuel our entire team for a week.

The Angelo Fields experiment was soon history.

Once, in desperation, I said, "Angelo, you know if you keep eating this way, you're going to die at a young age, don't you?"

He just looked at me and said quietly, "Yes I do."

GALE GILLINGHAM (G, 1966-'74, '76)

I remember how excited the coaches were when we selected Gillingham with our second choice in the first round of the 1966 draft. The coaches felt Gilly had the tools to become the best pulling guard in NFL history. He was a fabulous prospect—big and fast, with a tremendous work ethic.

Gilly lived up to those expectations, but unfortunately, by the time he had reached his prime, the Glory Years were over and the Packers were caught in a downward spiral. Even so, Gale was a perennial All-Pro.

He was a high-intensity type player, driven by a strong fear of failure. He was such a perfectionist that in his eyes he had to be errorless at every practice. He could not stand mediocrity. On Mondays after games—off-days for the players in those years—he would come into the training room for treatment and work himself into a frenzy in anticipation of the film sessions, in which coaches graded every player. Gilly almost always graded out very well.

In 1972, the decision was made to switch Gale from offense to the defensive line. I don't think Gilly was crazy about the idea, but he was not one to openly criticize a coaching decision, so he made the move.

Within two weeks, he suffered a season-ending knee injury.

Now, Gale never took anything for granted. He was diligent in his preparation for games—he was never late for a meeting, never missed a practice, never sloughed off during a film session. He thought everyone else should approach their jobs the same way.

Gilly's surgery was set for Tuesday morning, so at 11 p.m. on Monday, he called his doctor.

"Why are you calling me at this hour, Gale?" the doctor asked.

"Doc, on the nights before games, I have an 11 o'clock curfew so that I can perform at my best the next day," Gilly said. "I just wanted to make sure you were getting a good night's sleep. I don't want you screwing up my knee."

The surgery went well, but during his rehabilitation, Gilly expressed anger toward the organization. "I don't care if I ever play in Green Bay again," he told me. "Moving me to defense was a stupid decision."

He got over his bitterness and played for the Packers again, but he could not attain the level of performance to which he and the team had become accustomed. His competitiveness did not allow him to settle for being average, so he retired. One year later, Bart Starr lured him back to play a final season, but it was obvious that he just didn't have it anymore.

I've got a little story that illustrates Gilly's competitiveness. About five years after he retired for good, he called me and said, "You know, Dom, two or three days ago, my two boys challenged me to a game of H-O-R-S-E in the backyard. One of them made a dunk shot, so I went up and tried it."

You've got to remember Gale probably weighed 280 pounds at the time and was trying to dunk on a regulation 10-foot basket.

"I came down funny and hyperflexed my knee," he said. "Now, when I bend my knee, it seems like my muscle moves up my leg. What do you think is wrong?"

It wasn't difficult to diagnose the problem. He had ruptured his *rectus femoral* muscle and it had rolled up into his upper quadriceps.

"Gale, if it's been two or three days since this happened, you'd better go see an orthopedic surgeon," I told him. To this day, I don't know how he blocked out the pain.

Gilly saw a doctor, and my diagnosis was correct. He underwent surgery, and the last time I saw him—at his induction into the Packers Hall of Fame in 1982—he was still limping and using a cane.

Had that knee injury not cut down Gillingham in his prime, and had we been winners in the 1970s, there's no doubt in my mind that he would have been inducted by now into the Pro Football Hall of Fame.

DERREL GOFOURTH (C, 1977-'82)

Derrel was a good team player and a down-to-earth guy with a lot of common sense. He's another guy who paid a steep price physically for playing professional football.

One year, he hurt his knee with just a couple of games left in the season. He said it wasn't too bad and finished out the year. But a few weeks into the off-season, he called me and said, "My doggone knee is still sore. It feels kind of loose, too."

We flew him back to Green Bay and sent him to an orthopedic surgeon. Sure enough, he had a surgical knee. The damage was repaired and he came out in good shape. But Derrel had other problems, including early degenerative changes in his elbows, shoulders, and knees.

One day he came into the training room and said, "Domenic, I've got to tell you about my elbow. Yesterday, I went to grab a gallon of milk to pour it, and I could not lift it. I'm starting to worry about this a little."

Of course, I knew about his degenerative condition. There was nothing we could do about it. So I looked him straight in the eye and said, "Derrel, my best advice to you would be to start buying half-gallons."

He looked very perplexed for a moment, and then he burst out laughing.

Eventually, we advised him to retire, but he wasn't ready to call it quits. He wound up going to San Diego and playing two more seasons as a reserve for the Chargers. On the one hand, I was disappointed because I felt he was going to do more damage to his elbows. But on the other hand, I had told our coaches that we could prolong his career by bringing him off the bench, so it was somewhat satisfying to know that I was right.

JIM GRABOWSKI (RB, 1966-'70)

With all due respect to Jim Taylor, Grabowski might have gone down as the best fullback in Packers history had his career not been cut short by a knee injury. Grabbo was faster than Taylor, and probably a better pass receiver, too. And believe me, he hit the hole just as hard as Taylor.

Grabowski, a bruiser from the University of Illinois, spurned the advances of the Miami Dolphins and New York Jets of the upstart American Football League to sign with the Packers in 1966. He said he was thrilled to be a Packer, something we rarely heard out of players in the 1970s and '80s.

Grabowski and Donny Anderson entered the league together. They signed contracts with Green Bay that were worth more than $1 million combined, and their big salaries were a direct result of the competition for players between the leagues. Grabbo and Donny became known as the "Million-Dollar Backfield," or the "Gold Dust Twins."

There was little doubt about Grabowski's potential. However, midway through his second season, he injured his right knee and he was never the same runner again. He was hurt on a fullback option in a game against the Baltimore Colts when he tried to turn the corner and was tackled by Colts cornerback Bobby Boyd. He said he heard his knee pop; he was right next to the sideline, so he crawled off the field.

Grabbo didn't want to go on injured reserve. He continued to try to play, and re-injured the knee two or three times. Finally, he underwent surgery a week before Super Bowl II.

Total knee reconstruction wasn't being done yet and arthroscopic surgery was still the stuff of science fiction, so doctors repaired the damage as best they could. More than likely, Grabowski had torn his anterior cruciate or posterior cruciate ligament—or both.

Ironically, his injury helped make a hero of backup fullback Chuck Mercein, who made several big plays in our final drive in the famous Ice Bowl game.

EDDIE LEE IVERY (RB, 1979-'87)

Eddie Lee was the Packers' first-round draft choice in 1979 and was one of the most gifted running backs I've ever seen. He had tremendous speed and acceleration, great vision and awareness, and could cut on a dime. He was breathtaking during the pre-season of his rookie year, and the coaches knew they had something special.

As luck would have it, Eddie Lee suffered a knee injury in the '79 season opener against the Chicago Bears at Soldier Field. In his third carry as a professional, he planted his foot and his knee exploded. He suffered a torn anterior cruciate ligament and cartilage damage. It was a pretty good blowout, and many speculated that his career was over.

Eddie Lee was down in the dumps during his rehabilitation. But we kept encouraging him, pushing him, talking him up. I said, "Eddie Lee, even if you come back a step slower, you're still going to be better than most of the running backs in this league."

Finally, we made an impression on him, and he really went to work on that knee.

The next season, he was just starting to feel comfortable and get his rhythm back when we went down to Chicago and played the Bears at Soldier Field again. The date was Dec. 7, and we should have taken that as a bad omen. You guessed it. Another injury. Same knee.

This time, he tore the medial collateral ligament. Since his anterior cruciate had not been re-injured, we were still encouraged about his future. Eddie Lee went through another round of rehabilitation and did a good job of overcoming the psychological barrier of having suffered two injuries to the same knee.

Eddie Lee eventually resumed his career and became a very solid, dependable back. Every so often, he showed flashes of his old brilliance, but he had definitely lost a step. When he got caught from behind by a linebacker, he would lie on the turf and shake his head because he knew that without those knee injuries, he'd have been long gone.

Ivery ranks eighth on the Packers' all-time rushing list with 2,933 yards in 667 carries (a 4.4 average). And he ranks 16th on the team's career receiving list with 162 catches for 1,612 yards (10.0).

Just think what he would have done with two good knees.

EZRA JOHNSON (DE, 1977-'87)

Every so often a player comes along about whom you just get a special feeling. Ezra falls into that category. He was the kind of guy who was very appreciative of everything you did for him. He was friendly, cooperative, and coachable. And although he suffered through more than his share of injuries, he hated to miss practice. He was the type who would work his butt off to get back on the field.

Not many people know that Ezra had four surgeries in one calendar year; he had three back operations and one minor knee surgery. Yet, he missed only two regular-season games that year.

When Ezra came into the league as a first-round draft pick in 1977, he was a 229-pound defensive end. The coaches, concerned about his size, were thinking about moving him to linebacker, but he was tall and rangy and they decided to let him stay at defensive end and try to bulk him up instead.

Ezra had a lot of problems with his teeth, and we thought that maybe he wasn't eating enough because of them. So after the draft, the coaches kept him in Green Bay and arranged visits to a dentist to get his mouth cleaned up. Still, by the time training camp opened in July, he had put on only three pounds.

Dave Hanner was the defensive coordinator at the time, and he insisted that Ezra put on weight. He also insisted on monitoring the player by weighing him once a week. Hanner was pleased when Ezra quickly put on five pounds. Weeks later, he found out that Ezra had been putting a five-pound weight in his shorts before he stepped on the scale.

Eventually, Ezra did start putting on weight. By his third or fourth season, he was up to 262 pounds.

If it had been up to me, I would have left him alone. Ezra had 19½ sacks his rookie season, when he was still a lightweight. His forte was his explosive quickness, and I think he lost some of that after he put on 30 pounds.

When the team didn't renew Ezra's contract after the 1987 season, he was devastated. I was down about it, too, because Ezra was one of my favorites.

JERRY KRAMER (G, 1958-'68)

It is inconceivable to me that Jerry has not been inducted into the Pro Football Hall of Fame.

Ten of his former teammates and coaches have been inducted, and perhaps the voters feel that enough is enough. But no matter how you rationalize it, Jerry not being a part of that group is an injustice.

Kramer was a five-time Pro Bowl selection. He played on five NFL championship teams and two Super Bowl champions. He was the pulling guard who helped make the "Packer sweep" of the 1960s the most effective play in football. His blocking helped Paul Hornung, Jim Taylor, Elijah Pitts, and Donny Anderson pile up all those yards and touchdowns. And he threw one of the most famous blocks in pro football history, opening the hole for Bart Starr's winning touchdown in the Ice Bowl game.

Also, Jerry was a pretty good kicker who stepped in whenever our regular place-kicker went into a slump. He kicked 90 extra points and 29 field goals for a total of 177 points.

I'll never forget the field goal that Jerry made against the New York Giants that put the 1962 NFL championship game out of reach. The wind was whipping and the wind-chill factor—although it wasn't kept in those days—had to be somewhere around minus 50. Jerry kicked the ball on a low, line drive and it never went end-over-end; it spun counterclockwise and barely cleared the bar. Call it luck, call it whatever you want, but it was good and gave us a second straight world championship.

One would think Jerry would be bitter about the Hall of Fame slight, but that doesn't seem to be the case. I spoke with him at the Red Smith Dinner in Appleton, Wis., in 1992, and he insisted that it was no big deal.

"I've been asked that question a lot," he said. "I've pondered it a lot. It would be nice to be a part of the Hall of Fame. It would be nice to be with the guys. I'm introduced as a Hall of Famer many times, and it's a little embarrassing to have to say, 'Hey, I'm not in the Hall of Fame.'

"But there have been so many pluses in my career. The game has been so good to me. It's like I've gotten 500 presents under the tree and I'm upset that I didn't get 501."

Near the end of Vince Lombardi's reign, a reporter asked Jerry about what it was like to play for the famous coach in Green Bay, and he gave his famous "Camelot" response.

At the Red Smith dinner, I asked him about that response, and whether he looked at it differently now.

"The more I got away from the moment and the more I looked back at those times and those days, the more that comment seemed appropriate," he said. "It was a little bit like Camelot. It was one brief, shining moment. A moment that will never die."

Jerry is a successful businessmen and the author of two very good books about the Packers: *Instant Replay* and *Distant Replay.*

TIM LEWIS (CB, 1983-'86)

Tim, a first-round draft pick in 1983, was just starting to come into his own as a player when his career was cut short by a neck injury.

In a game against the Chicago Bears in Green Bay in 1986, Tim tackled wide receiver Willie Gault; the hit didn't seem to be particularly vicious, but Tim didn't get up.

For 5½ minutes, he was virtually paralyzed. He was conscious and talking, but he could not feel anything in his arms or legs. I feared the worst. It wasn't until after we got him on a stretcher and started rolling him off the field that he was able to start moving his hands.

"Dom, it's coming back!" he said. I was so excited for him, I became a bit emotional.

Tim underwent a Magnetic Resonance Imaging test, which revealed stenosis, a congenital condition in which the spinal column is unusually small; blows to the head, at certain angles, can compromise the spine itself. Tim had had two previous, less severe episodes of temporary paralysis.

It's a good thing the stenosis was discovered when it was; the next hit might have paralyzed Tim.

He had to retire, of course, and eventually wound up back at his alma mater, the University of Pittsburgh, where he is an assistant coach.

TONY MANDARICH (T, 1989-'92)

Coming out of Michigan State in 1989, Tony was considered a can't-miss prospect. He was 315 pounds of sculpted granite, a ferocious run-blocker who steam-rolled everything in his way.

The Packers drafted him without hesitation ahead of running back Barry Sanders of Oklahoma State. Everyone in the organization thought Tony would be entrenched as a tackle in Green Bay for a decade or more.

Contract negotiations were difficult. Tony traveled around the country, making the rounds on talk shows, and wherever he went he was critical of the Packers, Green Bay, and Wisconsin. It was not good public relations on his part.

Tony finally agreed to contract terms and reported to camp. And almost immediately, the coaches saw that he was not even close to being the player they expected him to be.

The first day that Tony put on pads, head coach Lindy Infante was supervising a seven-on-seven passing drill, but he was so curious about

Mandarich, he wandered over to watch Tony's first one-on-one block-ing drill. What Infante saw must have horrified him: The defensive linemen were flying past Mandarich so fast, it looked like his feet were encased in cement.

Obviously, Mandarich had gotten by on brute strength in college. His blocking techniques and footwork were far below NFL standards. He was an atrocious pass-blocker, and even his run-blocking—his bread-and-butter at Michigan State—was suspect.

The can't-miss superstar turned out to be the biggest of NFL draft mistakes: a first-round project.

Of course, there were persistent rumors that Mandarich was a steroid abuser in college. One story quoted an anonymous Michigan State teammate who said Mandarich not only was heavily into steroids, but that he also provided them to teammates.

It was rumored that Mandarich's prolonged contract negotiations with the Packers were nothing more than a stall tactic so he could rid his body of steroids and pass the NFL's drug tests. And indeed, he arrived in camp about 18 pounds lighter than he had been during his pre-draft workout with the Packers. His muscle definition and mass was not what it had been. He said he had dropped the weight to improve his foot speed, but many suspected the weight loss was a result of his going off the juice.

All I can say, in answer to the steroid rumors, is that Tony passed every steroid test that I administered. That's a fact. And he has con-sistently denied using steroids to bulk up. You can jump to any other conclusion, but it would be based on circumstantial evidence.

In his defense, Tony worked hard. He probably never would have become the dominant lineman that everyone thought he would be, but he might have become a decent player.

We'll never know. Tony suffered from post-concussion syndrome, then he developed a problem with his thyroid gland and lost even more weight. He dropped to 275 pounds—40 fewer than he weighed on draft day. And finally, he apparently lost his heart for the game.

The Packers eventually released him, and he will go down in the record books not as one of the all-time greats but as one of the biggest busts in the modern era of the draft.

CZESLAW (CHESTER) MARCOL (K, 1972-'80)

In March, 1987, I had the honor of presenting Chester for induction into the Packer Hall of Fame.

Just before I went into the banquet room for the induction ceremonies, a young lady stopped me and said, "Isn't it nice, what the Hall of Fame is doing for Chester?"

I was in a hurry and I didn't have a chance to reply. But I made sure to do that a few minutes later, when I presented Chester.

"The Packer Hall of Fame is not giving Chester anything," I said as part of my introduction. "If you checked the record books, you'd be surprised at the number of games this man won for us with his right foot. Chester Marcol deserves, and has earned, a place in the Packer Hall of Fame."

Chester, a soccer-style kicker who was born in Poland and went to tiny Hillsdale College in Michigan, was one of the most talented place-kickers I saw in my three decades in the NFL. He had a fluid, effortless kicking motion—his leg appeared to be limp on his follow-through—and the ball just exploded off his foot.

Marcol was drafted in 1972, and it was no coincidence that the Packers won the Central Division title that year. He connected on 33 of 48 field goals, led the NFL in scoring, was named rookie of the year, and made All-Pro.

Chicago Bears coach Abe Gibron so feared Marcol's kicking ability, he once assigned one of his special teams players to try to take Chester out of the game on kickoffs.

When he was questioned about that tactic, Gibron bristled and said something about Marcol being one of 11 players on the field. He added, "Who does he think he is, the Polish Prince?"

Marcol was so smooth, he could have been another Jan Stenerud in terms of longevity. I believe he could have been effective into the 1990s. Who knows how many records he would have broken?

Unfortunately, Chester got involved with alcohol and drugs. In my opinion, his downfall began when he opened a bar in Milwaukee in the early 1970s. It was a distraction Chester certainly did not need.

For years, the Packers organization knew Chester had a significant drinking problem. He went through many different modes of rehabilitation. We tried our best to keep him sober, but nothing was successful. Eventually, he began to experiment with hard-core drugs.

"I didn't know what a narcotic was until 1975," he told me. "I didn't know what cocaine was in 1978. Drinking made me vulnerable to other things."

In 1980, Chester was one of several Packers who were to make an appearance at the opening of a golf course in Rhinelander, Wis. When he didn't show, I became worried and I went looking for him, checking the area motels. I finally found him in mid-afternoon; he had been drinking and popping pills all day, and he was incoherent.

The Packers finally gave up on Chester in 1980 and released him. A couple of teams took a chance on him because of his enormous talent, but he was soon out of the league for good.

I lost track of Chester for about five years, but I know he eventually hit rock bottom. He went through a divorce and became destitute, and at his lowest point he actually drank battery acid.

Hitting bottom probably was the best thing that ever happened to Chester. He finally admitted he was powerless when it came to drugs and alcohol, and he began the day-by-day journey toward sobriety.

I was a little nervous when Chester asked me to present him for his Hall of Fame induction, because toward the end of his career in Green Bay, our relationship was quite strained.

Two days before his induction, I visited with Chester and his therapist. Some of the things I heard would make a grown man cry, and we did a little bit of that together. That meeting helped to restore some of the bonds that had been broken between us, and I'm happy to report that Chester and I get along quite well now.

The last time I talked to him, he was coaching football at a Class C high school in Houghton, Mich. I think that is probably the greatest thing he has ever done—to lower himself to that level for an opportunity to climb back into football.

There's no doubt in my mind that Chester will make an excellent coach. In the early 1970s, we didn't have a special teams coach per se; those duties were handled by other position coaches. Sometimes, Chester would take it upon himself to devise kickoff and kickoff return schemes. They were so effective, the coaching staff often would install them in the game plan.

KEN RUETTGERS (T, 1985-)

Ken has had a long, productive career with the Packers. He's the sort of tackle who doesn't overpower defensive ends but beats them by being fundamentally sound. He's a meticulous technician, a tireless worker, and a very intelligent player.

Kenny keeps a book on every defensive end he has faced in his career. He analyzes his opponents on film, charting and characterizing their moves and techniques so that he has an idea of what to expect in game situations. He even logs them by their personality type. In the off-season, he sticks to a strict regimen of four days of weightlifting each week, augmented by racquetball, basketball, karate, jumping rope, and hitting the speed bag.

Ken has been relatively healthy the last three seasons. But in 1991, he was hobbled by a nagging hamstring pull that he suffered in the fourth game of the season. It was a high pull, way up in the gluteus area, and it was slow to heal. He missed six games and then re-aggravated the injury on a running play in his first game back. Finally, he was placed on injured reserve and missed the rest of the season.

He caught flak from many of his teammates, who didn't believe the injury was that bad. Some of the players thought he was milking it, and there were a lot of things that were said about Kenny that were not necessary. I know he felt bad about not being able to play.

STERLING SHARPE (WR, 1988-'94)

Sterling might be the most misunderstood player who has ever put on pads for the Packers. He stopped talking to the media early in his career, and fans really never got a chance to know him. He shunned the spotlight away from the field, and as a rule he did not sign autographs.

Take it from me, though, Sterling was just as commanding a presence in the locker room as he was on the football field. He was cantankerous, mischievous, and boisterous, always needling his teammates. He loved picking on the guys who didn't play much, but it was all in good fun. Sterling was very articulate and witty, so anybody who tried to engage him in verbal horseplay usually ended up looking like a fool.

On the field, he was one of the toughest warriors I've ever seen. He played with all sorts of injuries—cracked ribs, pulled hamstrings, Achilles tendinitis, and even a painful turf toe that eventually required surgery after the 1993 season. Many times, he would not be able to practice all week, but you'd never know it on Sunday. People don't realize how difficult it is to perform in games without the benefit of practice. Sterling was one of a kind that way.

He never missed a game in his seven years with us, until a neck injury kept him out of our playoff loss to the Dallas Cowboys in 1994.

He had neck fusion surgery early in 1995, and his future is uncertain. If he does make a comeback, it will not be with the Packers. The two sides had a bitter parting when they could not agree on renegotiated contract terms for '95, while Sharpe was rehabilitating. He has vowed to play again, but I would strongly urge him to heed his doctors' advice. If they tell him it would be unwise to resume his career, it would be foolhardy to ignore them.

Sharpe caught 595 passes for the Packers, an average of 85 per season, for 8,134 yards. He caught 65 touchdown passes, including a career-high 18 in 1994.

Losing Sterling was a severe blow to the Packers. He's one of those guys you just don't go out and replace.

If the Packers can find a player who will give him two-thirds of Sharpe's production, they will have hit the jackpot.

JIM TAYLOR (FB, 1958-'66)

Jimmy didn't have Gale Sayers' grace or Jim Brown's speed, but boy, was he fun to watch when he carried the football. He was a punishing runner, the rare back who actually sought to initiate contact instead of trying to avoid it. In the open field, he simply lowered his head and tried to trample over linebackers or defensive backs who tried to tackle him. And when he smelled the end zone, it always took more than one guy to bring him down.

Jim still holds virtually every Packers rushing record: career yards (8,207); attempts (1,811); touchdowns (91); 100-yard games (26); most yards in one game (186); most yards in one season (1,474); and many more. He led the team in rushing for seven consecutive seasons (1960-'66) and finished his Packers career with an average of 4.5 yards per carry.

What stood out most about Jim, though, was that he was an amazing physical specimen. He was one of probably just a handful of players in the NFL in the early 1960s who lifted weights regularly. He lifted so heavily on Mondays, in fact, that he wasn't very fluid in practice the next two or three days. Vince Lombardi was a little concerned about that, but Jim performed so well on Sundays that Vince just left him alone. Very few players then had the muscle definition that you see on NFL players today, but Jimmy definitely was chiseled.

Taylor was way ahead of his time with off-season conditioning, too. Everybody else on the team dreaded Lombardi's grueling grass drills in training camp. Not Jimmy. While the other players were gasping for breath, Jimmy would actually be laughing.

Unfortunately, he and Lombardi did not have a happy parting. Jimmy played out his option after the 1966 season and signed with the expansion New Orleans Saints. Lombardi considered that to be an act of treason; afterward, he refused to refer to Taylor by name.

Taylor's running mate, Paul Hornung, retired after the '66 season, and during the off-season, Lombardi invariably was asked about the two.

"We will miss Paul Hornung," he would say. "The other fellow, we will replace."

KEITH UECKER (G-T, 1984-'91)

Keith was one of our Ed Block Award winners, given annually to the player who best exemplifies courage. I don't think we could have picked a better recipient.

In 1985, Keith had five operations on his left knee. While rehabilitating after the first surgery, he decided it would be an opportune time to have his Achilles tendon repaired. His Achilles had been injured the summer before his rookie season and it had bothered him ever since. We had to do a massive tape job on that ankle every day just to get him out on the field.

For the Achilles surgery, he went to a doctor in New Orleans on our recommendation. Before the operation was scheduled, doctors X-rayed Keith's chest, because he was complaining of pain and soreness and he had a lingering cold. They found the reason: pericarditis, a very serious condition in which the protective lining of the heart becomes infected.

Had Keith been anesthetized for the Achilles surgery, it could have been a life-threatening situation. He was put on antibiotics and was inactive for seven weeks, so he was unable to continue his knee rehabilitation program.

After the Achilles surgery, he returned to Green Bay and his knee had regressed. His range of motion had decreased, and he was in a lot of pain. Eventually, he required four subsequent surgeries that prevented him from playing at all in 1986.

Keith returned in '87 and started the first two games before the players strike. Then, in the first post-strike game, he stretched his medial collateral ligament and missed five games. Once again, he went through rehabilitation and returned to the starting lineup Dec. 6 against the San Francisco 49ers and helped revive our sagging running game.

Keith was not a natural athlete, but he worked extremely hard at it. His brutal off-season conditioning program included pushing a pick-up truck twice a week. I'm not sure I agreed with that type of training, but Keith felt it helped him maintain his leg strength.

One of the things I liked about Keith was that he genuinely felt bad about not being able to play while he was injured. He was receiving a pretty good salary from the Packers, and he was almost apologetic about it. You don't see that in too many players. Injury grievances are a fact of life in the NFL, but Keith publicly stated that he would never file one against the Packers. He was an honorable man.

ED WEST (TE, 1984-'94)

Ed came to the Packers as an unknown and unheralded free agent from Auburn, and right from the beginning I thought of him as a guy who probably was going to have a hard time making the team.

He had a great attitude, was a hard worker, played special teams and blocked very well. During a nutcracker drill during his first training camp, Ed lined up against veteran linebacker John Anderson and just destroyed him. "He basically buried me," Anderson admitted.

Paul Coffman, our starting tight end, said Ed played like a snapping turtle—once he got on you with a block, you couldn't get away.

There was just one problem: Eddie had hands of stone. That's fine for a boxer, but not for a tight end in the National Football League. Eddie just had a very hard time catching the ball. Passes skipped off his fingers, bounced off his palms, squirted out of his hands.

One day during practice, I happened to be standing on the sideline and he dropped a pass right in front of me. He walked over to me, frustrated.

"Damn," he said, "why am I dropping all these passes?"

I said, "Ed, I'm not a coach. I'm not an expert. But I was an end in high school, and I always made sure I looked the ball into my hands. You do not look the ball into your hands, Eddie. You look away just as the ball arrives. It's a bad habit, like a golfer who lifts his head just before he hits the ball."

He thought about that for a few seconds and then said, "OK, from now on, I'm going to look every ball into my hands, no matter what."

Well, for a while it was almost comical to watch Ed catch passes. He would look the ball into his hands, all right—and then stare at it for two or three seconds. That wasn't good, either, because he wasn't making many yards after the catch.

But he did start catching the ball and holding onto it. He made the team, and although he caught only six passes his rookie year, four went for touchdowns.

Ed has had a very nice career, with 202 receptions for 2,321 yards and 25 touchdowns.

Not bad for a free agent with suspect hands.

In an interview years later, Ed mentioned how I had helped him improve as a receiver. I was a little bit concerned that the coaches would not be real happy with a trainer instructing a tight end on how to catch a football.

I talked to Ed about that, and he said, "I don't care. It worked."

Early in 1995, it became obvious to Ed that the Packers had not included him in their plans for the coming season, so he signed a free-agent contract with the Indianapolis Colts. It's a good move for Eddie, because he'll play for Colts offensive coordinator Lindy Infante, the former Packers head coach.

But I wish he could have finished his career in Green Bay.

CHUCK WEBB, RB (1991)

Chuck was an example of a player who had a ton of natural ability, but lacked the mental toughness to overcome a minor knee injury.

He was a third-round draft choice in 1991, a running back who had had some problems on and off the field at Tennessee. Based on talent alone, he was projected to be a runner in the Barry Sanders mold. Chuck hit the hole so quickly in practices, you couldn't see his feet move.

However, early in the '91 training camp, he injured his knee and underwent arthroscopic surgery. The damage, thankfully, was minor. After some rehabilitation, Chuck started practicing again, but he complained about an inordinate amount of pain in the knee. His knee was stable. I'm sure he did experience some pain, but I believe he exaggerated it.

He started having second thoughts about a pro football career. I tried to tell him that he would be a millionaire someday if he would just keep working. I stressed to him that as his knee got stronger, the pain would diminish and he would regain his confidence.

He never gave it a chance. The Packers tried to trade him at the end of the season, but he retired instead. Naturally, everyone in the organization was disappointed with the Chuck Webb experiment.

Down the line, I think Chuck is going to regret his decision.

TRAVIS WILLIAMS (RB, 1967-'70)

Travis probably was one of the most gifted athletes ever to play for the Packers. And one of the most troubled.

Travis always seemed to be having personal problems, and he was terribly insecure. He had a ton of God-given talent, but he also had a deep-seated fear of failure.

Professional athletes are motivated by a variety of things: Money, ego, the will to win, competition. I think Travis was motivated by fear.

Often, while I was taping him before a game, he would say something like, "Dom, I don't know if I can do it today. I don't know if I have what it takes."

I would say, "What do you mean, Travis? You're probably the best athlete on the team."

And he was. Wow, could he fly. His nickname was "The Roadrunner," and it fit him perfectly. He was solid and compact, with powerful thighs and a fluid running motion.

When Travis was a rookie, he was prone to fumbling. Nothing infuriated Vince Lombardi more than a running back who did not protect the football. Vince reached the boiling point during a practice in which Travis lost the ball a number of times, and he ordered the rookie to carry a football with him wherever he went. For three weeks, Travis had to wrap his hands around a ball while he was watching film, while he was relaxing in his room, even while he was eating.

Travis cut down on his fumbles and became a very good running back. But, of course, he's better remembered for his ability to return kickoffs. He was, quite simply, the best kick returner in NFL history.

On Oct. 30, 1967, the rookie speedster from Arizona State ran back a fourth-quarter kickoff 93 yards for a touchdown to trigger a 31-23, come-from-behind victory over the St. Louis Cardinals.

Two weeks later, he returned kickoffs for 85- and 87-yard touchdowns in the same quarter against the Cleveland Browns. He added a 104-yard return against the Rams and finished his rookie season with a 41.06-yard average for 18 runbacks. More than a quarter-century later, that is still an NFL record.

Travis climaxed his rookie season by playing a prominent role in the Packers' 28-7 Western Conference playoff victory over the Rams. He rushed for 88 yards and two touchdowns, one of them on a 46-yard run.

Unfortunately, for Williams and the Packers, he never again approached those heights, although he did manage to lead the team in rushing in 1969 with 536 yards and a 4.2 average.

I think Travis, who was so fragile psychologically, lost some of his effectiveness after Lombardi decided to step down as head coach. Lombardi had so much confidence in Travis, he actually started to believe in himself. When Lombardi was gone, so was Travis' psychological crutch.

Ultimately, Travis became a victim of substance abuse. I knew, early on, that he was using amphetamines and diet pills (the players called them "up-time"). We made these pills available to any player who had a weight problem.

The thing was, Travis didn't have a weight problem.

Finally, I had to tell him, "Travis, there will be no more of those for you. You do not have a weight problem. I think you're using the pills for another reason."

He complied, but I suspected that he obtained pills from other sources and continued to use them.

The Packers traded Travis to the Rams in January 1971. He played one season in Los Angeles and returned a kickoff 105 yards for a touchdown, but a knee injury prevented him from playing in 1972, and he never played another pro game.

Plagued by drugs and later by alcohol abuse, the quality of Travis' life deteriorated markedly. His life also was marred by tragedy when his wife and the mother of their seven children died of drug-related causes at the age of 39 in 1985.

Travis died of liver and kidney failure on Feb. 17, 1991, in Martinez, Calif. He was 45.

When his daughter, Marla Williams, was asked what her father had been doing in recent years, she said, "I guess you could say slowly dying."

I knew, early in his career, that Travis had problems. We should have kept him in Green Bay, but in those days we just didn't have the resources to rehabilitate drug abusers. Drug testing was at least a decade away, and there were no substance abuse clinics.

For all his problems, Travis was one of the nicest, most decent men I have ever met. I never heard him say a bad word about anybody. I truly loved him, not only as a football player, but as a person. When I heard he had died, I broke down and cried.

Chapter 8

The Sorry Years

If the Green Bay Packers were the National Football League's measuring stick in the 1960s, then it is fair to say that they were the league's laughingstock in the 1970s and '80s.

"The Pack Will Be Back," became pro football's version of "the check is in the mail." Year after year of losses and excuses and empty promises piled up like so much garbage in a junkyard.

When you work for an organization that is as successful and proud as the Packers had been under Vince Lombardi, then failure—and miserable, consistent failure, at that—is much more difficult to stomach.

Unfortunately, the franchise became very adept at accepting defeat. If losing is an acquired taste, then we developed a hearty appetite for it in the 1970s, and we continued to gorge on it in the '80s.

It shows in our record. Since 1967, the Packers have won exactly one division title and have won ten games in a season just twice. Those are the cold, hard numbers.

Before Mike Holmgren became the head coach in 1992, we had five winning seasons in a 24-year span. Our combined record in those years was 146-201-9.

How did it happen? How did such a great franchise fall so far?

The short answer is that our players got old and we didn't replace them at the right time and with the right people. We tried to make up for our deficiencies with trades, and made more mistakes. Slowly but surely, we became talent bankrupt. And to compound those errors, we got some bad breaks—and made our share of poor picks—in the draft. Also, there were a few instances when we had the money to spend on good players, but we were too salary-conscious to part with it.

Put it all together, and you've got the blueprint for a long and ugly drought in the NFL.

At some point, the Green Bay Packers ceased to be a feared opponent and began to be looked at as a break in other teams' schedules. The franchise was seen as unappealing by star players coming out of college—the city was too small, the weather too cold, the facilities substandard, the opportunities for income outside the game virtually nonexistent.

Losses mounted and morale declined. There were times that I worried about the future of the franchise. In 1988, I approached some members of the Executive Committee with my fears, and they did not reassure me. They hinted that the board of directors might have to get together and start talking about trying to find a corporation to take over the team and possibly even move it. I walked away convinced that the Green Bay Packers were in serious trouble. If not for Lindy Infante's 10-6 season in 1989, my worst fears might have come true.

Personally, it was a humbling experience to be associated with those losing teams. I had been spoiled—as had most of our fans—by the 1960s.

We were all in for a rude awakening.

Packer-bashing became quite popular in the 1970s. I can't say we didn't deserve it, but a lot of it was pretty vicious stuff. One sick idiot even went so far as to shoot Dan Devine's dog.

I have to admit, though, that some of the jokes might have been funny if they hadn't hurt so much. Here are a few of the better ones I've seen and heard over the years:

"On a Sunday afternoon, Packer fans in a bar looked up to see a man walk in with a dog under his arm. The man sat on a stool and put his dog on the bar. 'No pets in the bar,' the bartender said. 'This is no ordinary dog,' the man replied. 'He's a real Packers fan, and when they score, he does amazing things.' Sure enough, when the Packers kicked a field goal, Rex turned a somersault on the bar. After a touchdown, Rex did cartwheels down the length of the bar. 'Geez, that dog is really something,' the bartender finally admitted. 'What does it do when the Packers win?' The man scratched his head. 'Darned if I know,' he said. 'I've only had him three years.'"

Or: "Why is Lambeau Field a safe place in a tornado? Because there are never any touchdowns there."

Or: "A man found an antique lamp and rubbed it, and out popped a genie. When told he had one wish, the man asked for world peace. The genie pondered the request, then asked the man for an atlas. 'There are so many countries, I think world peace is beyond my powers,' the genie finally said. 'Do you have another wish?' The man replied, 'Get the Packers into the playoffs!' The genie scratched his head and said, 'Can I see that atlas again?'"

Or: "The judge in a divorce proceeding takes the little boy aside and asks, 'I suppose you'll want to live with your mother, right?' The youngster shakes his head and says, 'Not on your life, judge. She's always beating me.' The judge says, 'Well, then, you prefer to live with your father?' The boy says, 'Heck, he beats me, too.' The perplexed judge says, 'Then where do you want to live?' And the boy says, 'Can I go live with the Green Bay Packers? They never beat anybody.'"

Or: "The Packers were playing so poorly during one game that fans in the stands could be heard yelling, 'Hey, up in front!'"

Or: "Warden to condemned criminal: 'We're going to give you a choice. You can go to the chair, or you can choose to watch Packers games every Sunday for the rest of your life.' Criminal to warden: 'Electrocute me. At least that only hurts for a little while.'"

Or: "An announcement was made over the radio in Green Bay one Sunday afternoon: 'Will the lady who left her 11 children at Lambeau Field please come pick them up? They're beating the Packers, 14-0.'"

Or: "An interesting crime statistic could be the start of a trend. It seems a lot of people with Green Bay Packers jackets no longer want them and are using guns to force others to take them off their hands."

Or: "I have a problem. I have two brothers. One plays for the Packers and the other is sentenced to die in the electric chair. My two sisters are ladies of the night and my father sells drugs. I recently met a girl who was released from a reformatory, where she was doing time for smothering her illegitimate child to death. I love this girl, and I want to marry her. My problem is this: Should I tell her about my brother who plays for the Packers?"

During the Sorry Years, the joke almost always was on us.

In another time and another place, Phil Bengtson probably would have had considerable success as a head football coach. He was the architect of the stingy defenses that had played a major role in the Packers' five NFL titles.

From 1960-'69, Bengtson's defenses held opponents to an average of 15.6 points per game. His best season may have been in 1962, when the Packers gave up just 148 points in 14 regular-season games.

Bengtson was a fine coach, but succeeding Vince Lombardi, who had turned Green Bay into the football capital of the universe, was an impossible act to follow.

Lombardi recognized in 1967 that the end of his championship run in Green Bay was near, and he thought he was getting too old to rebuild the team a second time. So he stepped down as head coach, kept his general manager title, and turned over the coaching duties to Bengtson.

Poor Phil was doomed from the start. In 1968, he inherited a roster full of aging stars who had run out of goals. The Packers won their first game under Bengtson, but finished with a 6-7-1 record—their first losing season in 10 years.

At that point, Phil probably should have cleaned house and started over. But he felt a tremendous loyalty to players such as Ray Nitschke, Elijah Pitts, Dave Robinson, Bart Starr, and Travis Williams. These were guys who had won championships. What was he supposed to do—trade them to the Bears?

The Packers rebounded to an 8-6 record in 1969, but there was more losing in 1970 and Bengtson, under pressure, turned in his letter of resignation before the last game of the season. The Packers finished 6-8 in his final year and 20-21-1 in his three seasons. That was the best record of any coach in the post-Lombardi era until Holmgren, who was 27-21 going into the 1995 season.

Bengtson died on Dec. 18, 1994, at the age of 81. He won't be best remembered as a head coach, perhaps, but that doesn't matter. He was a class act, and a winner. I know it, and so does everyone who was associated with the Packers in the 1960s.

Dan Devine was hired on Jan. 14, 1971, to succeed Bengtson. Devine had an excellent record at Arizona State University (27-3-1) and the University of Missouri (93-37-7), but he was a quirky, eccentric man and fans and players in Green Bay never really warmed up to him.

After he left, Devine said that when he had tried to discipline players, they went to the Executive Committee and whined. The members of the committee sided with the players, Devine claimed. "You can't win when ownership sides with the players," he said. He also said that if he had to do it all over again, he would have gotten rid of everybody in the organization except the trainer (me) and the equipment man (Bob Noel).

I think he meant it as a compliment.

In his first year, Devine used the Packers' first-round draft pick to select John Brockington, the bruising running back from Ohio State. In 1972, Devine drafted a talented cornerback named Willie Buchanon in the first round and a kicker named Chester Marcol in the second.

Those players formed the cornerstone of what should have been a dynasty.

In '72, Brockington rushed for 1,027 yards, Buchanon earned the Bert Bell Trophy for defensive rookie of the year and Marcol led the league in scoring with 128 points. With the recently retired Bart Starr calling the plays from the sideline as an assistant coach, the Packers went 10-4 and won the Central Division title.

In a divisional playoff game against Washington, Starr wanted to open up the offense against a Redskins defense that was obviously bent on stopping Brockington. But Devine stubbornly refused to throw the ball, and the Packers lost, 16-3.

The next year, Starr was gone and the Packers slipped to 5-7-2. I think one of Devine's biggest mistakes was changing quarterbacks early in the season. We had won the Central Division title with Scott Hunter at quarterback, and then we beat the New York Jets, 23-7, in the season opener. But Devine traded for Jim Del Gaizo, a left-handed quarterback with the Miami Dolphins, and inserted him as the starter. That destroyed Hunter and fragmented the team.

The move backfired further when Del Gaizo was critical of Devine, calling him the worst coach he had ever seen.

It was to be Del Gaizo's only season with the Packers, but the quarterback problem remained. Devine went into the 1974 season desperate to produce a winning record, but he had little confidence in Jerry Tagge, a Green Bay native who had led Nebraska to two national championships. And Hunter was no longer with the team.

So on Oct. 22, one day after a 10-9 loss to the Chicago Bears, Devine traded five high draft picks to the Los Angeles Rams for 34-year-old quarterback John Hadl.

One of our linebackers, Jim Carter, called it the "Lawrence Welk trade," because we had given up "a 1-2, a 1-2-3." It was, and still is, the worst trade in the history of the Green Bay Packers. Hadl had been a fine quarterback in his prime, but he already was over the hill when we got him. And the loss of five critical draft choices wound up crippling the Packers for many years.

Following the '72 season, Devine had said, "We have built our team without sacrificing our future." He could no longer make the same boast.

The 1974 season was a disaster as we stumbled and bumbled to a 6 8 record. Dissension tore the team apart. Most of the players were down on the coaching staff as a whole and disliked Devine in particular, and it was obvious by their performance on the field. They simply gave up, scoring only 23 total points in the last three games, all losses.

That stretch easily was the darkest period of my 32 years with the Packers.

The low point came before our final game against the Falcons in Atlanta on Dec 15. A few people in positions of power in the organization got together with some players and made plans to boycott the game. Several players actually were going to skip the team flight to Atlanta and force the Packers to forfeit.

I got wind of these developments and did what I could to persuade the players not to follow through with their plan. I told them it would be suicidal to their football careers and would jeopardize the team's future in the NFL.

At the very least, it would have been the blackest mark in the history of the franchise. It was just an asinine idea. Can you imagine something like that happening today?

Fortunately, cooler heads prevailed and the boycott fell through. The players went through the motions and lost to a poor Falcons team, 10-3.

Within a week, Devine resigned. The executive committee moved quickly to hire a new coach, and on Dec. 24, 1974, Bart Starr was named to lead the Packers back to the promised land.

It was an emotional decision on both sides. Starr was revered in Green Bay, and the Executive Committee conveniently overlooked the fact that he had no coaching experience, except for the one season he had served as an assistant to Devine.

Starr's friends tried to talk him out of taking the job because, quite frankly, it was not a golden opportunity. The team was looking at a long rebuilding process, thanks to Devine's trade for Hadl. Morale had plummeted to an all-time low.

Starr welcomed the challenge. Years later, he admitted that he was naive enough to believe that he could reverse the team's fortunes within a few years.

Bart agreed to a three-year contract as coach and general manager. In hindsight, the Executive Committee probably should have hired a general manager and let the inexperienced Starr concentrate on coaching the team.

Because of his inexperience, Bart often leaned on other people in the organization instead of trusting his instincts. He often told me later, "I wish I had followed my gut."

I will say for the record that I thought Bart was an average coach at the beginning, but that he improved each year. He so desperately wanted to succeed; he really poured himself into the job. On many occasions, I arrived at the office at 6 a.m., and found that Bart already had been there for two hours, watching film. You know how presidents seem to age dramatically during their terms because of the burden of their responsibilities? That was Bart. He was consumed by the job, which was in truth more like a mission to him.

If you looked at Bart's won-lost record of 55-77-3 (.410), you would conclude that he did not succeed in turning the franchise around. But I guarantee that at the end of his nine-year run, he probably was one of the better coaches in the NFL.

Bart's No. 1 priority in 1975 was somehow to reverse the plummeting morale and eradicate the cancerous depression that had spread throughout the organization.

Devine had left the team in a shambles. Many players coming out of college in the mid-1970s stated publicly that they would play anywhere but Green Bay. I remember how frustrated I would get when I would be taping a player before practice and he would say, "God, if I can just get out of here and go someplace else . . ."

I used to tell those guys, "You know, your attitude is what's making this situation worse. I think if you would just upgrade your attitude a little bit—and if everybody else would do the same—then maybe we'd win some of these games we're losing. Laying there and feeling sorry for yourself, that's not going to prove anything or accomplish anything."

But by then, losing had become contagious. We had players who were fiercely competitive and hated to lose, of course, but too many others came into the training room the day after a loss and acted indifferent about it. They just weren't affected. This was the environment into which Bart stepped.

He was determined to restore some feeling of pride in being a Green Bay Packer. He held a team meeting and talked about attitude, stressing the importance of the players' approach to the game and their approach to life.

"From now on," Bart told the team, "when I say, 'Good morning, how are you?' I want you to say, 'Great. Everything is fine,' instead of the things I've been hearing around here. I ask how people are doing and I hear, 'Oh, all right, I guess.' "

Bart was a good motivator, but I think he made the mistake of believing that all players would seize the opportunity to play professional football the same way he did. Unfortunately, not many players have Bart's total dedication, along with his ability to overcome pain and adversity and his desire to improve. The simple truth is, many of his players cheated him in those areas.

Bart had just four picks in the first eight rounds of the draft in his first season, thanks largely to the John Hadl trade.

He also had a number of other problems. Our best player, All-Pro linebacker Ted Hendricks, who had blocked seven kicks in 1974, became a free agent and could not come to terms on a contract. For $100,000 more, we could have kept a Hall of Famer. But the organization didn't want to spend the money, so Bart traded him to the Los Angeles Raiders for two first-round draft choices.

There were other problems. Cornerback Ken Ellis, unhappy with his contract, walked out of camp twice and was fined and suspended. Bill Lueck, one of our best offensive linemen, requested to be traded, and Bart sent him to the Philadelphia Eagles for a fourth-round draft choice.

In the season opener, the Detroit Lions blocked three of Steve Broussard's nine punts to set an NFL record. Chester Marcol tore a quadriceps muscle and was lost for the season. The next week, cornerback Willie Buchanon suffered a broken leg against Denver.

We started the season with four straight defeats. Syndicated columnist Steve Harvey ranked us No. 1 in his "Bottom Ten," and wrote, "Packers coach Bart Starr is off to his worst start since 1955, when he helped quarterback Alabama to an 0-10 season."

We finished 4-10 in Bart's first season, 5-9 in his second and 4-10 again in his third.

Bart expended a lot of energy during those years putting out fires off the field.

In 1975, Ellis demanded to be traded and was part of the deal that brought quarterback Lynn Dickey to the Packers. Bill Bain walked out of camp after a film session and was traded the next day. John Brockington, the record-setting running back, also asked to be traded but by then he had slipped so badly that the team found little interest in him league-wide.

In 1977, the Packers lost a pre-season game, 38-3, to the New England Patriots, and Starr accused Patriots coach Chuck Fairbanks of running up the score. From there, things got worse. Brockington was placed on waivers after gaining 25 yards in 11 carries in the season opener. Linebacker Gary Weaver and Dickey were lost to injuries, the latter for the second successive year. Wide receiver Ken Payne was suspended and fined for insubordination when he responded with an obscenity to an assistant coach's order to move closer to the team bench in the final minutes of a 17-7 loss to the Cincinnati Bengals.

By 1978, Bart had finally gotten rid of most of the head cases, and the Packers put together a winning record: 8-7-1. It wasn't good enough to get into the playoffs, but it was the team's best season since '72. There were other signs that the Packers were back on track. The '78 draft was the team's best in many years, producing wide receiver James Lofton and linebackers John Anderson and Mike Douglass. And second-year running back Terdell Middleton rushed for 1,116 yards—to this day, the best total by a Green Bay runner since Brockington's 1,144 in 1973.

The Packers added talented running back Eddie Lee Ivery in the 1979 draft, and going into the '79 season, Green Bay fans were optimistic that the team was on the verge of returning to glory.

It was not to be. Ivery tore up his knee on his third carry of the season, the first of ten serious injuries that tore apart the team's foundation.

Lofton had a run-in with Starr after the coach called three running plays in the last 1 minute 41 seconds of regulation, with the score tied 21-21, in a game against Minnesota. The Packers lost, 27-21, in overtime, without ever getting the ball. A few weeks later, Lofton made an obscene gesture to the fans after dropping passes and fumbling away a potential touchdown in a 27-22 loss to the New York Jets.

We slipped to 5-11, and when the season ended, Starr fired our defensive coordinator, Dave Hanner, after Hanner declined to submit a letter of resignation. Hanner had spent 28 years with the organization.

After starting the 1980 season with a 0-4-1 pre-season record, Starr was starting to feel some serious heat. But he vowed not to resign and received a vote of confidence from team president Dominic Olejniczak.

A 12-6 victory over the Chicago Bears in the season opener was followed by humiliating losses to the Detroit Lions (29-7), Los Angeles Rams (51-21), and Dallas Cowboys (28-7). By then, Dickey was publicly questioning whether he was the right quarterback to lead the Packers out of oblivion. The low point of the season was a 61-7 loss to the Bears on Pearl Harbor Day.

Starr was relieved of his general manager duties on Dec. 27, following a 5-10-1 season. I think that was the worst thing the Executive Committee could have done. Players begin to doubt a coach who isn't supported by management. Tom Landry's early Dallas Cowboys teams had terrible records, but each year his contract was extended. That showed the Cowboys they had to work up to Landry's expectations instead of sitting back and waiting for a coaching change.

Despite the setback for Bart, he led the team to an 8-8 record in 1981. Once again, it appeared that we were headed in the right direction.

The 1982 season was sort of a fluke because it was shortened to nine games by the players strike. We went 5-3-1 and made the playoffs for the first time in ten years. Our offense, with a healthy Lynn Dickey throwing strikes to James Lofton, John Jefferson, and Paul Coffman, could score from anywhere on the field.

We beat the St. Louis Cardinals, 41-16, in the first round of the playoffs before losing to a very good Dallas Cowboys team, 37-26.

It was to be Bart's finest hour.

We regressed to an 8-8 record in 1983, and the day after our regular-season finale, a 23-21 loss to the Chicago Bears, Starr was fired by team president Robert J. Parins.

Starr said that Parins came into his office and said rather bluntly, "Bart, you are relieved of your duties as head coach." Parins then turned and walked out, according to Starr, who closed his door, buried his head in his hands and let the emotions of nine losing seasons pour out.

I'll be the first to admit that Starr didn't have a good record. But the man had literally dedicated his life to the Green Bay Packers. He was the driving force behind the construction of the team's indoor practice facility. He was a leader in the community and was involved in many charitable projects.

There is no good way to fire a man, but Bart deserved better than that cold slap in the face.

As the search began for a coach to replace him, the perception around the state and in the organization itself—right or wrong—was that the next coach had to be a disciplinarian and a taskmaster. I never understood what people meant when they said they wanted a "tough" coach; any player who went through one of Bart's camps would tell you his practices were torture. I approached Bart many times and suggested that he cut back because I feared the players were leaving their games on the practice field. Starr was not soft in any way, but his public demeanor and his reputation as a gentleman probably made it appear otherwise.

At the same time, the team's board of directors couldn't resist the idea of having another of Vince Lombardi's disciples lead the team. Forrest Gregg, the great offensive tackle whom Vince Lombardi had once called "the finest player I ever coached," seemed to be just the man for the job. Gregg, a no-nonsense coach, had taken the Cincinnati Bengals to Super Bowl XVI. And the challenge of bringing the Packers back to their former greatness appealed to Gregg.

On Christmas Eve, 1983, Gregg officially was named head coach, agreeing to a five-year contract.

Gregg was tough, all right. Training camp two-a-days were sheer torture for the players. Gregg believed in full-pad, full-contact practices, even though that had not been Lombardi's style. And he was tough on the team in other ways. During one stretch of heartbreaking defeats, a reporter asked Gregg if he was worried about his players' morale. I'll never forget his answer: "Their morale? I'm not worried about their morale. They'd better be worried about mine."

Unfortunately, Forrest's tenure in Green Bay coincided with the rise of the Chicago Bears, who would compile a 50-13 regular-season record and win Super Bowl XX while Gregg's Packers were going 25-37-1 during the same span.

Forrest hated the Bears, and he disliked Mike Ditka, their pompous coach who had a habit of shooting off his mouth and gloating a bit too much after victories. Iron Mike took obvious pleasure in beating Green Bay, probably because of the Bears' inability to do so in the '60s—when Ditka was their tight end and Gregg was starring for the Packers.

We all believed that Ditka's idea to use 350-pound defensive lineman William "The Refrigerator" Perry as a fullback was at least partially the result of a desire to humiliate Green Bay. At any rate, we certainly helped make Perry a national celebrity, not to mention a millionaire. He scored his first NFL touchdown against the Packers, bowling over our undersized linebacker, George Cumby, at the goal line. In another game, he caught a touchdown pass against us, which was the ultimate insult.

I think Forrest's overemphasis on the Bears rivalry probably hurt the team a little in the long run. We simply could not beat Chicago, and we invested too much emotion trying. The players would be fired up for Bears games, but we couldn't match up with them talent-wise. Pride, determination, and preparation can overcome a lot, but in a matchup of superior talent vs. marginal talent, the superior talent will win 90 percent of the time.

And that was pretty close to Forrest Gregg's winning percentage against the Bears. We beat Chicago once in eight attempts under Forrest, and lost the last six. He became almost obsessive about it, and his frustration carried over to the players. I hated to see us resort to late hits and cheap shots. Charles Martin's infamous body-slam of Bears quarterback Jim McMahon a full three seconds after the whistle blew was an embarrassment.

Partly because we couldn't beat the Bears, Gregg was never able to get his team over the .500 hump. After back-to-back 8-8 seasons, his 1986 team slipped to 4-12 and his '87 team went 5-9-1.

Forrest resigned on Jan. 15, 1988, to become the head coach at his alma mater, Southern Methodist University. He left behind a team that was not much better, from an overall talent standpoint, than the one he inherited.

As I mentioned earlier in this chapter, at this point I was extremely worried about the future of the franchise. I talked about my fears with Tony Canadeo, a Packers Hall of Famer and a member of the board of directors, and he agreed that the credibility and viability of the franchise had been severely compromised by years of ineptitude.

It was a very troubling period.

The Packers targeted Michigan State coach George Perles to be their next coach. Perles' offensive philosophy revolved around the running game, which was attractive to the Packers because of the inevitably difficult weather conditions in Green Bay in November and December. But Perles, it turned out, was only using our organization to get a sweeter deal at Michigan State.

And so, the Packers turned to their second choice, Cleveland Browns offensive coordinator Lindy Infante. Nineteen days after Gregg resigned, Infante became the tenth coach in Packers history, agreeing to a five-year contract that called for him to share personnel decisions with Tom Braatz, the executive vice president of football operations. Lindy had had just one year of head coaching experience—and that in the United States Football League—but he was regarded as a brilliant and innovative offensive coach.

"We will get a system installed and then find out how the players can respond to that system," Infante said.

He quickly found out the answer: Not well.

Lindy was flabbergasted and frustrated by what he saw in early practices. One day, after we had gotten into the pre-season, he came down to the training room and I could see the frustration on his face. He was nearly in tears.

"Coach," I told him, "the only thing that this team lacks right now is 15 good players."

He didn't agree with me. Right up until the ax fell on him, he consistently defended his players. I can understand a coach doing that, but I think there comes a time, when the mistakes keep piling up, that you stop defending them and start benching them, trading them or releasing them.

Looking back, I think that was Lindy's only real weakness. He was blindingly loyal to his players. He hated to let anybody go; I think it hurt him personally. If he had cut a few more players, however, he might have won a few more games. Who knows?

The players struggled to pick up Infante's complex offense, and we wound up with a 4-12 record in 1988. If not for season-ending victories over Minnesota and the Phoenix Cardinals, it would have been our worst season since Ray "Scooter" McLean's 1-10-1 record 30 years earlier.

Before the 1989 season, the Packers invested heavily in the league's new Plan B free agency system, signing nearly two dozen Plan B players to contracts. The talent came together magically—or perhaps I should say Majik-ally. Quarterback Don Majkowski, the Majik Man, stepped up to have the one brilliant year of his career, completing 353 of 599 passes, both club records that have since been broken by Brett Favre.

Majkowski, along with a supporting cast of several fine, young players, led the Packers to a 10-6 record, our best in 17 years. Along the way, we upset the defending Super Bowl champion San Francisco 49ers, 21-17, in San Francisco.

We also swept the hated Bears. The first victory, in Green Bay, will always be known as the "instant replay game." Majkowski's winning touchdown pass to Sterling Sharpe with 32 seconds left was at first ruled incomplete because an official said Majkowski had crossed the line of scrimmage before releasing the ball. After a long delay, Bill Parkinson, the replay official, overruled the original call on the field, and the touchdown stood.

Sharpe, our emerging second-year wide receiver, led the NFL with 90 receptions in 1989, the first Packer to do that since Don Hutson in 1945. Brent Fullwood, our talented but enigmatic fullback, had the best year of his career, rushing for 821 yards. Linebacker Tim Harris had 19½ sacks and became the first defensive player since Ezra Johnson in 1978 to be selected to play in the Pro Bowl.

We shared the National Football Conference Central Division title that year, but the Minnesota Vikings advanced to the playoffs because of their better division record.

The outlook was bright going into the 1990 season, but it dimmed in a hurry. Eighteen veterans, the majority of them starters, missed the first day of training camp because of contract problems. These guys apparently believed that because they had had one decent season— remember, we didn't even make the playoffs—management should have ripped up their contracts and made them all millionaires.

Majkowski held out for 45 days before signing a club record $1.5 million contract. Offensive lineman Ken Ruettgers, Ron Hallstrom, Rich Moran and Alan Veingrad missed a combined 101 days of practice.

Lindy wanted to teach these guys a lesson. He wanted to prove to them that they couldn't hold a gun to the Packers. Lines in the sand were drawn, and they dissected the team. There was a great deal of animosity and bitterness between players and management.

There was no way we could succeed in that environment. We gave up a team-record 62 sacks in 1990 and averaged only 85.6 rushing yards per game, the worst output in franchise history.

We also had problems hanging on to the ball in '90. At halftime of one game, Lindy stood up and said, only half-joking, "OK, the strategy for the second-half kickoff is for us to line up, receive the kick . . . and then I want everybody to fall back and recover the fumble."

The crushing blow in a 6-10 season occurred on Nov. 18, in a game against the Phoenix Cardinals. Majkowski was flushed from the pocket and was sacked by defensive end Freddie Joe Nunn. Don hurt his right shoulder, and at first the injury was diagnosed as a deep bruise.

When the soreness lingered for a month and did not respond to treatment, Majkowski sought a second opinion. Dr. Gary Losse of San Diego found a damaged rotator cuff and operated on Dec. 13. Not many throwers—baseball pitchers or football quarterbacks—have come back all the way from rotator cuff surgery. And although Don worked diligently at his rehabilitation, he never was the same player again.

We lost six of our first seven games in 1991 and slipped to 4-12— our third 4-12 record in six seasons. Tom Braatz was relieved of his duties on Nov. 20. Exactly one week later, Ron Wolf, the director of player personnel for the New York Jets and a veteran of 29 years as a pro football scout and executive, was named executive vice president and general manager by Bob Harlan, the team president.

Wolf was given full authority to run the Packers' football operation. The handwriting was on the wall for Infante, who was forced to coach under a microscope. The pressure was intense, but Lindy held up well. He never lost faith in his ability or in his assistants. In fact, he went into Wolf's office and told his new boss in no uncertain terms that he was a hell of a coach and that, if given the opportunity, he would get the job done.

We lost three straight games after Wolf arrived, but we rebounded to beat the Minnesota Vikings, 27-7, in the season finale. The players presented the game ball to their emotional coach. Almost everyone knew by then that Infante was gone.

Three days before Christmas in 1991, Wolf fired him and let his entire staff go.

Right up until the end, however, Infante was classy.

"I've worked hard and I've been dedicated to the team and to the community," he said. "When you spend yourself as I have, and as the coaching staff has, to accomplish lofty goals and you're willing to step out there and put your neck on the line and do everything you possibly can to get that done, you can look anybody in the eyes. But most importantly, you can look yourself in the mirror and say, 'I gave it everything I had.' And that's the way I feel.

"If it isn't written in the cards for me to reap the benefits of the hard work we've put in here, then so be it. But I'm not walking away from this thing with my head down. I'm not walking away from here with anything less than the knowledge that I gave the absolute best. I can live with that."

At Infante's last meeting with the players, he told them they were not far away.

"As this team goes on and has success in the future, I'm going to feel like I'm a little bit a part of it, selfishly," he told them. "I'm going to feel very much like I had something to do with it."

Lindy obviously can be proud of the 1989 season, but I think he can be equally proud of the way he handled himself and the team in '91. Somehow, despite all the adversity and distractions, Lindy held the players together. I still don't know how he did it; I don't know what he used for adhesive. But there was no finger-pointing going on, no undermining, no back-stabbing.

Infante remained positive to the end. That rubbed off on the players, who were willing to accept some of the blame for the mounting defeats. I found that to be quite remarkable. Usually, when things are going badly for a team, the players spout off to the media and blame the coaches, the owners, or even the fans. That wasn't the case with Lindy's players. Until the last minute of the last game, they were positive.

Although Wolf wanted to start anew, I'm sure he had at least some mixed feelings about firing Infante, who was very popular in the community. Lindy and his wife, Stephanie, were involved in more charitable activities than any coach we'd ever had. They were community oriented people. Certainly, Ron was aware of the positive things Lindy had done as far as community relations. But unfortunately, it comes down to the bottom line in professional sports: Winning is the only thing that matters.

My relationship with Lindy had its rocky moments. We did not get along well at first, and we had our share of disagreements. For example, we did not see eye-to-eye on the need for a full-time strength coach. Our weightlifting and conditioning programs had fallen behind those of other NFL teams, and I told Lindy exactly that after the miserable 1990 season.

"Lindy, we need a guy who is going to be downstairs working with the players at all times," I said. "We need him to be in the office, so he is a part of the team."

He disagreed.

"I don't think we need a full-time strength coach," he said, "because so few of our players stay in Green Bay in the off-season."

"They will stay if the program is a good one," I argued.

I went to Tom Braatz and told him the same thing. Finally, out of frustration, I went to Bob Harlan, the team president. Within a few weeks, the Green Bay Packers hired their first full-time strength coach.

On at least a couple of occasions, I seriously considered giving my letter of resignation to Lindy. At one point, our relationship became so strained, we scheduled a meeting to try to resolve our differences. The night before, I told my wife and children that I might be coming home the next day unemployed.

We met at 6 a.m., had a great talk and sort of cleared the air. I admire Lindy for the way he handled that situation—he kept our disagreements private, and I don't think anyone else in the organization even suspected that we were having problems.

Although Lindy and I did not always have a smooth relationship, we developed a mutual respect for one another. Over a period of time, I grew to admire him and his abilities. When he left, it was an emotional parting on both sides. I had hoped Wolf would give him one more year to prove himself, but Ron had his own agenda and I certainly understood that.

Lindy wound up on his feet, and I couldn't be happier for him. He is the Indianapolis Colts' new offensive coordinator, and he will do well there.

At the time of Lindy's firing, many longtime Packer fans had become cynical and distrustful of the organization. And who could blame them? Outside of a few fleeting moments of success, we had been losers for nearly 25 years.

We needed fresh blood, a new start, a different perspective.

In Wolf, we had someone who could give us that.

Chapter 9

The Future Is Now

In the days after Lindy Infante's firing on Dec. 22, 1991, it quickly became apparent that former New York Giants coach Bill Parcells was Ron Wolf's No. 1 candidate to become the 11th coach in Packers history.

Other names were mentioned—Pete Carroll and Dave Wannstedt, who would go on to take head coaching jobs with the New York Jets and Chicago Bears, respectively, were prominent among them.

But there was no denying the fact that Parcells was the man Wolf wanted to hire.

Looking back at the whole Parcells fiasco, I still get mad at the guy. He had left the Giants for the television booth because of a heart condition, and it was obvious that he had no intention of returning to coaching at that time. He had strung along the Tampa Bay Buccaneers before stranding them at the altar—turning down a deal worth millions and complete control of the team—and now he was toying with the Packers.

Had he been honest, I think he should have discounted himself as a candidate immediately. But I think he liked the speculation and intrigue because it gave him something to talk about on his pre-game and halftime shows during the NFL playoffs.

When it became apparent that Parcells would not be headed to Green Bay, Bob Costas asked him why he had backed off from the job. Parcells' answer was that it had never been formally offered to him. Well, that might have been true, technically, but it was obvious that the job was his for the taking. Money certainly was no object, and Wolf would have involved Parcells in all football decisions.

No, the simple truth was that Parcells wasn't ready to return to coaching. He knew it all along, and he should have had the guts to come out and say so.

In the wake of the Parcells farce, Mike Holmgren, the San Francisco 49ers' offensive coordinator, emerged as the top candidate.

As San Francisco's quarterbacks coach in the mid-'80s, Holmgren had been instrumental in the development of Joe Montana and Steve Young. In 1989, his first season as offensive coordinator, the 49ers had the NFL's top-ranked offense. During his six years with the Niners, they compiled a .753 winning percentage and won back-to-back Super Bowls in 1988-'89.

On Jan. 11, 1992, Wolf made it official, announcing Holmgren as the Packers' new head coach.

I spent only one season with Mike before I retired, but what I saw made me wish I was ten years younger. As a trainer, I had more input in Mike's program than I had had under any other previous coach.

For instance, I knew our record at home had been poor for many years, but when I added up the numbers, it was worse than I thought: 60-67-2 from 1975 to 1991. I told Holmgren and Wolf that I thought the team might benefit from being sequestered in a hotel on the nights before home games, and they went immediately to team president Bob Harlan and Mike Reinfeldt, the chief financial officer.

The Packers were sequestered in a hotel before home games in 1992, and they went 6-2 at Lambeau Field and Milwaukee County Stadium.

Mike made another change that I was happy to see. I'd always felt that Packers teams, since the end of the Lombardi era, worked too hard and too long in their practices.

Many people thought Vince was a tough coach—and certainly in many ways he was—but he did not believe in contact during both sessions of two-a-days. It was always shorts in the morning, pads in the afternoon.

But Bengtson, Devine, Starr, Gregg, and Infante all had their teams hitting twice a day during training camp. Injuries mounted, and players never had a chance to rehabilitate them properly. Criticism of the training staff and medical staff increased, but a lot of things were out of our control. The players were expected to be on the field, and they were expected to hit twice a day. Period. There is no doubt in my mind that many of our teams went into the regular season dog tired and leg weary.

Holmgren changed that, and it was like a breath of fresh air. The 49ers had spent a fraction of the time in pads that we had in recent years, and nobody was calling them wimps.

I had some very favorable impressions of Mike during my one season with him. I think he is a real player's coach. He is honest and fair, and he treats his players like men. He commands respect—and gets it—but he also seems to have a great deal of compassion for the guys who play for him.

After three straight 9-7 seasons and back-to-back playoff appearances, it appears certain that Mike has a long and bright future in Green Bay.

I'm very confident that we finally have turned the proverbial corner that Bart Starr talked about back in the mid-1970s.

Holmgren and Wolf work very well together. Holmgren has input in personnel decisions, but they are ultimately made by Wolf, who is a shrewd judge of talent. As an example, how many other NFL executives projected Brett Favre to be one of the league's top quarterbacks when he was languishing on the Atlanta Falcons' bench in 1991?

And to his credit, Wolf recognized that, in Holmgren, he had a coach who would be able to tap Favre's enormous potential.

Just look at the great draft picks Wolf has made: Robert Brooks (third round) and Edgar Bennett (fourth) in 1992; and Mark Brunell (fifth) and Doug Evans (sixth) in '93 are but a few. His 1994 draft could still turn out to be a great one if first-round pick Aaron Taylor and third-rounder LeShon Johnson overcome injuries and fourth-rounder Gabe Wilkins continues to develop.

Bob Harlan is not as visible as Holmgren and Wolf, but he is every bit as important as the team continues to improve and shed its image as a perennial loser.

Harlan's steady climb upward in the organization's power structure was impressive. He originally was hired by Dan Devine in 1971 as an assistant general manager. He was named corporate general manager in 1975, corporate assistant to the president in 1981, and executive vice president of administration in 1988.

He was elected as the team's president on June 5, 1989, replacing Judge Robert J. Parins. Once elected, the team's new chief executive officer wasted little time initiating his first major project. In August, 1989, Harlan announced plans to construct 1,920 club seats and 36 private boxes in Lambeau Field, an $8.3 million expansion which increased the stadium capacity to nearly 60,000.

In 1991, convinced that the team was treading water competitively, he relieved executive vice president Tom Braatz of his duties and one week later hired Wolf.

Harlan also has been instrumental in the construction of the Don Hutson Center, the state-of-the-art indoor practice facility that replaced Bart Starr's original building. He has brought the Packers into the 20th century in terms of marketing and merchandising.

And, in what was an unpopular move with many Packers fans from Milwaukee but unarguably is in the team's best interests, financially and competitively, Harlan in 1994 ended the team's tradition of splitting home games between Lambeau Field and Milwaukee County Stadium.

I feel bad about the faithful Milwaukee fans who have stuck with the Green Bay Packers through thick and thin, but I think those fans will be happy with the result in the won-lost column. Lambeau not only is the finest football facility in the country, but it's very tough on opponents. Especially warm-weather opponents. Especially in December.

With Wolf and Holmgren calling the shots and Harlan intelligently guiding the franchise, I am confident that the Packers are on the verge of returning to their place among the very best organizations in professional sports.

Nobody will be pulling for them more than me.

Chapter 10

Packers Notebook

Years ago, we were headed back to the airport after playing a game in Detroit.

In those days, the team's chartered buses could pull right up to the plane on the tarmac, so the players wouldn't have to walk through the airport.

Our driver was trying to maneuver the bus as close to the plane as possible, and she backed right into the wing and ruptured it. There was a pretty big tear.

A few minutes later, two guys pulled up, propped a ladder against the wing and took out a roll of duct tape. And damned if they didn't patch the hole in the wing with that tape!

Astonished, I watched them do their job, as did several of the players. Finally, they got the ladder out of the way, the engines started to whine and we took off. I was nervous as hell, and so were the players.

One of them whispered to another, "Good thing that didn't happen while we were in the air."

Willie Wood enjoyed telling the story about a friend who lived in Los Angeles but had always wanted to attend Ole Miss. This was during the 1960s, remember, when racial tension throughout the country was high.

Willie recommended that his friend attend college closer to home. "Ole Miss is not a good spot to be at this time," Willie advised. "You'd be better off finding a school in California."

The young man insisted. It was Ole Miss or nothing.

"So I finally got him a scholarship to Ole Miss," Willie concluded, "as a javelin catcher."

One night during training camp, Vince Lombardi ran into a player who was returning to the dorm at St. Norbert College just before curfew.

Vince sized up the player and growled, "You're half-drunk."

The player nodded sheepishly.

"Yeah," he said, "I ran out of money."

In 1961, Vince decided to take the team to Dallas a few days before we were to play the Cowboys. He thought the team would benefit from practicing in warm weather.

Vince wasn't happy with one of the practices, however, and he put the players through a grueling grass drill in which they ran in place with their hands up in the air. It was a hot, sticky day, but he made them run for nearly 15 minutes.

Members of the Dallas media couldn't believe what they were seeing. After practice, the reporters gathered around Vince. "We've never seen that drill before," one of them said. "Was that some kind of punishment?"

"No, no, that was not a drill," Vince said. "That was the Italians practicing for World War III."

I attended a National Athletic Trainers Association convention in 1972, two years after Vince died. One of the seminars was led by two so-called sociologists who argued that Lombardi was a bad role model.

They criticized his "archaic" approach to discipline and regimentation. They said people should be able to do whatever makes them feel good, whether it was taking off their clothes in public, stomping on the American flag, or burning their draft cards.

I filled with anger as I listened to their nonsense. Those clowns were attacking Vince and everything he stood for, everything that made those 1960s Green Bay Packers teams so great.

The seminar was held in a hall that was filled with a thousand trainers from around the world. There were microphones in the aisles so the sociologists could answer questions at the conclusion of their program.

I couldn't wait that long. I rushed to one of the mikes and started yelling at them. They yelled back, and it became quite a screaming match.

And then something wonderful happened. Other trainers rushed to the mikes in a spontaneous and unanimous show of support for me. We literally drove those sociologists from the stage. It gave me great satisfaction to see them walk off with their heads hanging.

The NFL has strict rules on what sort of jewelry a player can and cannot wear during games. Normally, those rules are enforced to the letter.

That's why I could never understand how Reggie Roby, the Miami Dolphins' fine punter, could get away with wearing a wristwatch during games in the 1980s.

I was worried that one of our players would go in to try to block a punt, get his finger caught in the band and have it ripped off. It was a legitimate concern.

I complained to the officials before games, but they never did anything about it. I wrote several letters to the league and never got a reply.

It took me a long time to figure out why: Don Shula, the Dolphins' coach, was on the NFL rules committee. Shula was, and is, a powerful figure on that committee. A letter from the trainer of the Green Bay Packers was not going to get anywhere with that group.

And so, Roby got to wear his wristwatch.

Two nuns came from Milwaukee to observe practice for a few days in 1991. They were Samoan, so they were big fans of the two Samoans on our roster: Esera Tuaolo and Vai Sikahema.

I ran into them in the public relations office one day and asked, "Have you sisters been praying for the Packers this year?" We were 3-11 at the time.

One of them said, "Oh, yes, we pray for you before every game."

I took one of her hands, flipped it palm up and said, "Now, look, we've lost 11 games. If you were praying really hard, you'd have bead burns on your fingers."

Vince's wife, Marie, never missed a Packers game, home or away. She always sat next to Vince on the team plane.

Once, the pilot inadvertently left his microphone on, and everything he said could be heard in the cabin.

He must have been talking to the co-pilot when he said, "Wouldn't it be great to have a beautiful blond and a beer right about now?"

The players roared, but the flight attendants were horrified, and one of them—a blond—rushed up the aisle to tell the pilot to turn off the mike.

Marie Lombardi grabbed her by the arm as she ran by and said, "Don't forget the beer."

I'll never forget the first time that Lombardi's Packers played the Paul Brown-coached Cleveland Browns. The game was played in Cleveland, on Oct. 15, 1961.

Brown was regarded as a genius in football coaching circles. Lombardi respected him immensely, and I think he saw the game as a sort of personal measuring stick.

It was easy to tell when Vince was especially concerned about an upcoming game. He became more agitated and intense; he nit-picked and flew off the handle at the slightest mistake.

Vince put the team through an unusually tough week of practice.

The day before the game, he called the team together and said, "Men, tomorrow we will be playing before a crowd that is greater in numbers than the entire city of Green Bay. They'll be screaming their heads off and looking for the Browns to beat our butts. Let's come out here prepared to win the football game."

The team was ready to play. We whipped the Browns, 49-17.

The lasting memory I have of that game is of Vince starting to run across the field to shake Brown's hand when it was over. But Brown never acknowledged him; he made an about-face and ran into the locker room. I'm pretty sure that stung Vince quite a bit.

Although Brown didn't like losing to Lombardi, he respected Vince's coaching skills. Years later, Brown threw a reporter out of a press conference during training camp because he remembered the writer's magazine article that depicted Vince as a cruel, heartless taskmaster.

"If you don't have more respect for a person of Vince Lombardi's stature, you don't belong in this group of sports reporters," Brown told him. "I will not go on until you leave."

The reporter got up and left.

The 1967 NFL championship game between the Packers and the Dallas Cowboys in Green Bay often is referred to as the "Ice Bowl." The temperature at game time was minus 16 degrees.

But that day was balmy compared with the conditions the Packers faced in the 1962 championship game in New York, against the Giants.

I was raised in Hurley, Wisconsin, so I know what cold weather is. But this was ridiculous. The game was played before wind-chill factors were recorded, but I swear it had to be minus 50. The wind was gusting so hard, it kept blowing over the wooden benches on the sidelines.

At halftime, the players huddled in the "locker room" at Yankee Stadium, which was nothing more than a cement-block area underneath the stands, with a dirt floor.

Most of them curled up in the fetal position to try to stay warm. Some of them were so cold and so frustrated they were actually in tears. We were very fortunate that nobody suffered a serious case of frostbite.

I shivered all the way home on the airplane, and the players were cuddled up in blankets. That had to be the coldest game in the history of the franchise.

If the 1967 game was the Ice Bowl, then the '62 game should have been called the North Pole Bowl.

Another thing that stands out about the 1962 championship game was that our outstanding safety, Willie Wood, was ejected for bumping a referee.

Willie had made a brilliant play and broken up a pass, but the official was not in great position and threw a flag for defensive pass interference. Willie jumped up to argue the call and he sort of bumped the official, who immediately ejected him.

Willie was not the kind of player who would intentionally bump a referee. He was devastated. I remember him standing on the sideline, shivering despite the heavy coat draped over his shoulder pads. Tears were streaming down his face. I've never seen a player, before or since, so broken up by an official's call.

Although the '62 championship game was the coldest, the Ice Bowl wasn't exactly a day on the beach.

It was so cold that Dallas' great wide receiver, Bob Hayes, inadvertently telegraphed plays when he came to the line of scrimmage. If the play was a run, Hayes shoved his hands into his pants because he knew he wouldn't have to worry about catching a pass.

In the early 1960s, Willie Wood's locker was right next to the training room door. Every day after I showered, I made sure Willie wasn't around and then I grabbed his deodorant and put a little squirt under each arm. I would laugh to myself because I didn't think he had any idea that I was raiding his deodorant supply.

One day, Willie poked his head into the training room and held up an empty can.

"Hey, Dom," he said, "it's your turn to buy."

Willie once got bowled over by a huge running back, who crashed into the end zone, collided head-first with the goal post, and was knocked senseless.

When he came to a few seconds later, Willie was bending over him.

"Are you OK?" Willie said.

"Yeah, I guess so," the player responded.

The quick-thinking Wood said, "Well, that was little Willie warning you that if you ever try to get by me again, I'll clobber you harder than I just did."

Jack Vainisi, a scout for the Packers in the 1950s and '60s, tells this story about Max McGee, and swears it's true:

"I had heard of a guy in New Orleans, attending Tulane, who was supposed to be an outstanding player. His name was Max McGee. I decided to go down to Tulane and interview McGee before the college draft to see what kind of person he was. We had heard rumors that McGee was a night owl; that he liked to go out on the town and buy drinks for the ladies.

"I got into town very late, about 1:30 a.m. I went to the Tulane campus and found Max's dorm. I tried to get in but the doors were locked. But I noticed some of the second-floor windows were open, so I hollered up, 'Does Max McGee live here?'

"Somebody yelled back, 'Yes, just open the door and put him inside. We'll take care of him.' "

Speaking of Max, he likes to tell the story about when he was young and very single, and had a date with a woman who lived on the second floor of an apartment building.

One night she was running late. She let Max in and told him that she would be ready in a few minutes.

Well, the woman had a dog, and the dog's favorite toy was a little rubber ball. Max started bouncing it against the wall, and the dog, tail wagging, chased it and retrieved it.

Then Max accidentally bounced the ball through an open window. The dog bounded up on the windowsill and jumped.

Max was frantic. How would he get out of this one?

When the woman finally came out of the bathroom, Max looked up at her and solemnly asked: "Has your dog been depressed lately?"

Bart Starr was out with an injury one game and backup quarterback Zeke Bratkowski was sent in.

On the first play, Zeke threw a perfect spiral that hit Max right in the hands, but he dropped the ball.

"How the hell could you miss that one?" Bratkowski asked Max in the huddle.

"I'm not used to those kind of passes," Max responded. "Bart usually throws them more wobbly and down around the ankles."

In a related story, we were playing the 49ers in San Francisco in an important game late in the 1962 season. Bart threw a perfect pass to McGee on third down, but the ball went right through his hands. It would have gone for a sure touchdown, because there were no defenders within 10 yards of Max.

Lombardi was going out of his mind on the sideline. None of the players knew what to say to Max as he trotted off the field.

He looked around at everybody, shrugged and said, "Boy, that smog sure is rough out there today."

Some players wear corset-like braces to alleviate strain on their lower backs.

Once, one of our players came into the locker room and started to undress. His locker buddy looked up and casually asked, "How long have you been wearing a girdle?"

The player responded, "Since my wife found it in the glove compartment."

Dom Moselle played football for Hurley (Wis.) High School, Superior State, and the Green Bay Packers. When Dom was a little boy, he said, he wrote a letter to God asking for $50 so he could buy a new bicycle.

Some people at the post office thought Dom's letter was cute and decided to forward it to President Dwight D. Eisenhower.

Ike read the letter, felt sorry for Dom and sent him a crisp $5 bill.

Moselle wrote back to God: "Thanks for answering my prayer, God. But it's just like those bastards in Washington—they deducted $45."

Henry Jordan came from a small town that had a tiny, one-runway airport. Once, Henry had to fly back to Green Bay during the off-season and was waiting for his flight.

The airport didn't even have a tower. Henry sat down next to the controller, a friend, and struck up a conversation.

After a few minutes, the controller turned his microphone on and said, "Flight 292, come in from the north."

He and Henry talked for another minute or two, and he turned his mike back on and said, "Flight 416, come in from the south."

Jordan tapped him on the shoulder and said, "Do you realize that you have one plane coming in from the north and one from the south?"

The controller grabbed his mike and said, "Y'all be careful now, y'hear?"

Jordan, God bless him, loved to tell the story about the day Lombardi halted a thunderstorm during training camp.

"We had a longer meeting than usual, figuring we'd never get out on the field to practice," Jordan said. "Lombardi was pretty unhappy, walking around wringing his hands and fretting about the lost practice time.

"Finally, he looked up at the heavens and shouted, 'Stop raining!' There was a huge clap of thunder and a flash of lightning, and the rain stopped.

"I'm a hard-shelled Methodist," Jordan would say, "but I've been eating fish every Friday since then."

I was visiting a friend in the hospital and Jordan also was there, visiting his wife, who had just given birth. We stopped to chat in the hallway and in the course of congratulating him I happened to mention that our team physician, Eugene Brusky, had 14 children—and they were all single births.

Henry couldn't believe it. He kept slapping his leg and saying, "No way, no way." It took some time for me to convince him that I was telling the truth.

Later, as I was leaving the hospital, Jordan poked his head out of his wife's room and yelled—loud enough for the whole hospital to hear, I'm sure—"Hey Dom, you tell Dr. Brusky that he's either a darned good Catholic or he's a sex maniac!'"

On Sunday morning before the 1967 NFL championship game against the Dallas Cowboys, several members of the team joined Vince Lombardi at mass.

Paul Hornung was there, as were Gary Knafelc, Bob Skoronski, Max McGee and a few others. I was there, too.

When the ushers came around for collection, Vince threw a $5 bill into the basket, so all the players wisely decided that that was the way to go. Everyone threw in $5.

At the end of the mass, the ushers started walking down the aisle again with the collection baskets.

Max, who was not Catholic and didn't quite understand the concept of a second collection, poked Hornung in the ribs and said, "What are they going to do, search us now?"

I remember one game when one of our players was limping around pretty badly on the field. Lombardi barked at me, "Get out there and see what's wrong with him."

Back in those days, if a trainer stepped onto the field, a timeout was charged to the team. So I reminded Vince, "Coach, if I run out there, it's going to be a timeout."

Lombardi thought about that for a second and then turned his attention to the limping player.

"Hey," he screamed, "get off that field!"

Early in my career, I was trying to catch up on some rest during two-a-days at training camp, so I decided to lie down on the training table during the lunch break between practices.

Lombardi wasn't crazy about people lounging around, and no sooner had I lay down than he came bursting into the training room.

I jumped to my feet, heart racing, and started to stammer out an excuse.

Vince just gave me one of his smirks and said, "Go ahead, lay down. Better you than a player."

One day a salesman came in with a brand new diathermy machine and made a deal with Vince. We got the diathermy machine, which emits a high-frequency electric current that stimulates injured tissues beneath the skin. The salesman got a handful of Packers tickets.

Vince was sold on the fancy new machine, so naturally he was going to sell it to the players.

As they wandered innocently past the training room, he would yell, "Hey, come in here and try out this machine. It will take care of any injury you've got. Knock the pain right out of you."

The player would sit in the machine for about 10 minutes, get up and shrug his shoulder or flex his knee and say, "By gosh, coach, it does feel a lot better."

Then Jimmy Taylor walked past.

"Hey, Jimmy," Vince said. "You want to try it?"

Jimmy eyed the machine warily.

"Coach," he said, "I just walk by that machine and I feel a hell of a lot better."

Vince once decided that he wanted to cut down on the use of a certain four-letter word in the locker room area and on the practice field.

He put a big jar in the training room and said, "Any time anybody uses that word, I want him to throw 50 cents in the jar."

Most of the guys thought it was a pretty good idea. Ron Kramer, though, rebelled. He didn't see eye-to-eye with Lombardi about a lot of things, and the "cuss jar" was one of them. Ron wasn't afraid to speak out, because he was one of the few players who wasn't intimidated by Lombardi. He frustrated Vince at times, but he was a heck of a player.

Anyway, Ron came in the training area one day, repeated the forbidden word ten times in a row and threw $5 in the jar, just to spite Vince.

There is a misconception about Super Bowl I that seems to have been accepted as fact, and I'd like to set the record straight. It is said that Lombardi was not concerned about our opponent, the Kansas City Chiefs, because he believed that there was no way the Chiefs could beat his superior Packers.

Nothing could be further from the truth. Vince was as nervous before that game as I had ever seen him.

In 1992, I was watching one of the NFL playoff games when I heard Will McDonough, a reporter for NBC-TV, mention casually that the Packers hadn't even bothered to scout the AFL championship game between Kansas City and Buffalo before Super Bowl I. That's not true. Jack Vainisi, our top scout, was at the game.

McDonough also said that when reporters asked Lombardi after the game what he thought about the Chiefs, Vince supposedly said something to the effect that the Chiefs were not in the same class as the Packers.

McDonough went on to say that he visited with Chiefs coach Hank Stram after the game in Stram's hotel suite, and passed on Lombardi's comment.

"Did Lombardi really say that?" McDonough said a peeved Stram told him. "Did he really say that?"

The truth of the matter was, when we were out in Santa Barbara, California, preparing for the game, Lombardi was a nervous wreck. He felt a great deal of pressure because the Packers were representing the established NFL against the upstart AFL.

In the days leading up to the game, he got dozens of calls of support from NFL coaches and representatives.

I overheard a conversation Vince had with Chicago Bears coach George Halas, and I remember Vince saying, "Well, George, we're going to do our best. I know the pressure is on us, and God help us."

I know Vince didn't take the Chiefs lightly, so I also know that none of the players did.

Jack Concannon, a quarterback who had played five seasons with the Chicago Bears, joined us in 1974. He was with the Packers for only one year, but he made a big impression on me.

Concannon was a skinny guy, but he was one of the roughest, toughest players I've ever been around.

One evening, late in the season, it was snowing and blowing as the players left practice. Concannon lived about 10 miles out of Green Bay and on the way home, his car skidded out of control and struck an overpass.

He came in the next morning, and his face was so swollen I didn't recognize him. I told him that he had better get over to the hospital to get some X-rays, because I was afraid he had broken some facial bones.

"Do you have a headache?" I asked him.

"Hell, I've always got a headache," he said.

He walked out of the training room, and I assumed he left to go get checked out. But about 15 minutes later, he walked back in wearing his football pants, shoulder pads and jersey. Then he stood in front of the training room mirror and tried to put on his helmet. He had to use his fingers to literally stuff his face into the cage. I don't know how he withstood the pain.

Concannon went out and practiced that day, and he didn't miss a practice the rest of the week.

Nate Borden was the only black player on the team from 1955-'59. He was a hard-working defensive end who was good at knocking down the interference. He and Max McGee became good friends and hung around together quite a bit.

One weekend in late November, Nate wanted to visit friends in Appleton. He didn't own a car, so he borrowed Max's. When Nate returned to Green Bay, the streets were slick from an ice storm. He turned a corner too sharply and Max's car started spinning out of control, hopped a curb and smashed through the plate-glass window of a furniture store.

There Nate was, sitting in Max's car—in the middle of a living room display.

Nate called the police, and then called Max, who arrived at the store a few minutes later.

As Nate explained the whole story, Max stood in the furniture showroom with his hands on his hips. Nate kept apologizing, and Max finally said, "Aww, don't worry about it, Nate. But what are we going to do with all this second-hand furniture?"

At the height of his fame and popularity in Green Bay, Don Majkowski went to Los Angeles during the off-season for a few days of vacation. He hung around with several L.A. athletes and even mingled with a few celebrities.

Majkowski and some of his friends were out on the town one night, and somebody brought a beautiful blond to their table.

"I'd like you to meet the Majik Man," he said, introducing Majkowski.

She looked Majkowski up and down and said, "Listen, punk, there's only one Magic in L.A., and he plays basketball."

In the pre-season Hall of Fame game in 1980 in Canton, Ohio, a thunderstorm rolled overhead while we were playing the San Diego Chargers. By the fourth quarter, I could see that the lightning strikes were very close to the stadium.

I went up to coach Starr and said, "Bart, we've got all these television wires and cables all over the place and the players are wearing spikes. This could be a dangerous situation. I think you'd better talk to somebody."

Bart conferred with the officials, who agreed to suspend the game with 5 minutes 29 seconds left and the score tied, 0-0.

We huddled in the locker room, and about 15 minutes later we got word that the lightning had subsided and that the officials wanted to resume the game.

I didn't think it was a good idea.

"Bart, the players have been in here 15 minutes now," I said. "They're stiff. This is an exhibition game. There's no point in going out there again."

Eventually, the officials agreed to call the game, and it went into the history books as the only game in Packers history suspended by lightning.

There were rumors going around during the time Bart was coaching that his son, Bret, was using cocaine, and possibly even sharing it with a couple of the players. I know Bart was greatly distressed about this.

I approached him one day and said, "Coach, let's put these rumors to rest. With your permission, I'll search the entire locker room and dressing room areas. If there are any illegal drugs anywhere in this building, I'll find them."

We met on a Saturday before a game, when the Packers offices were empty. With Bart supervising, I opened every single locker. I looked into every nook and cranny of the building for any sign of drugs. I couldn't find anything that looked even remotely suspicious, and Bart was relieved.

Unfortunately, Bret Starr did have a drug problem. In 1988, Bart had the tragic misfortune of discovering his son's badly decomposed body in Bret's suburban Tampa, Fla., home. According to the medical examiner who performed the autopsy, traces of cocaine were found in Bret's body and caused his death. He was 24.

The entire Packers community grieved with Bart and Cherry. They held up well publicly, but I know it tore them apart.

We had a player for a while who missed more practices than he attended. There was always something wrong with him.

On the outside of the doctor's door, the players' various allergies were noted on a pharmaceutical cabinet. This particular player was allergic to several different foods and medicines.

One of his teammates penciled in another allergy on the bottom of the list: "Practice."

Of the hundreds of injuries I saw over the years, a few bordered on the ridiculous.

One day before practice, one of our players said, "Dom, I've got a bad hamstring."

"Did you hurt it at practice yesterday?" I asked.

"No," he said. "My wife had a baby last night and I think I hurt myself while I was helping her in the delivery room."

I just had to laugh about that one.

At the annual NFL combine for college players who are eligible for the draft, hundreds of athletes are poked, prodded, measured, weighed, and put through drills and strength tests. They also are given a 50-question intelligence test called the Wonderlic.

Doctors are on hand to check the players' necks and range of motion in their joints. I'll never forget the time a doctor told one of the prospects, "Jump up on the table."

The player thought the doctor was putting him through some kind of agility drill. So the guy, from a standing start, leaped onto the table.

If he didn't demonstrate much intelligence, at least he showed he had a good vertical jump.

Ben Agajanian, a place-kicker, joined us for the 1961 season because Paul Hornung had been called up into the service. Ben was one of the NFL's early specialists. He had a special kicking shoe, and he was the first guy I'd ever seen who had an electric sock to keep his kicking foot warm.

Vince Lombardi told him, "Ben, the only reason you're here is to kick. Don't worry about anything else."

Agajanian took Vince at his word.

After he kicked off—usually while the ball was still in the air— he started running toward the bench.

Epilogue

I have many fond memories of the players and coaches with whom I worked over the years, and I have enjoyed telling their stories in this book. But I would be remiss if I did not mention some very special people who worked behind the scenes and never got enough credit.

Carl "Bud" Jorgensen was an employee of the Green Bay Packers for 47 years, from 1924 through 1970. Bud was an equipment man at first, then went on to serve as the head trainer for 25 years. He did not have any formal medical training; he learned on the job, by trial and error. And he was terrific.

Bud had an encyclopedic mind when it came to athletic training, and he was always willing to share his knowledge and expertise. I learned something from him every day. He was a great person to work with, and a very dedicated employee of the Packers.

Bud was inducted into the team's Hall of Fame in 1976.

Gerald "Dad" Braisher was the equipment manager for many years. Dad was a bachelor, and it was not uncommon for him to show up for work at 7 a.m. and leave the stadium at 10 or 11 p.m.

Dad was a company man through and through. After the players put new cleats on their shoes, they dumped the old cleats in wastebaskets. At night, Dad turned over the wastebaskets and picked out the cleats that were in good enough shape to re-use.

One year, he wanted Vince Lombardi to buy wool dickeys to help keep the players' necks warm. Vince saw the expense as extravagant, and denied Dad's request.

"Absolutely not," Vince said. "We're not going to spend our money on something like that. It'll just spoil the players, anyway."

So Dad went out and bought the dickeys—50 of them—with his own money. That's just the kind of guy he was.

Bob Noel replaced Braisher as the head equipment man in the mid-60s. Before that, Noel had worked for many years as Dad's assistant. In that capacity, he was not officially an employee of the Packers and did not get paid. Yet he was an extremely dedicated worker. He would come over during his lunch hour or on his days off and help Dad with the equipment.

Bob attended all of the games at Lambeau Field, and he also traveled with the team to games in Milwaukee and Chicago, where he slept on the training room table because the team could not afford to pay for an extra hotel room.

You just don't see dedication like that anymore.

Bud, Dad, and Bob were the kind of people who helped make the Green Bay Packers a unique organization in professional sports.

The Packers are the only publicly owned, non-profit major sports franchise in America. A total of 1,877 stockholders own 4,632 shares in the corporation, and I am proud to say that I am one of those stockholders. I own exactly one share.

The corporation is governed by a seven-member Executive Committee, elected from a 45-person Board of Directors. There is no single team "owner." This sort of corporate set-up will never again occur in professional sports.

The Executive Committee's main duties are to approve capital expenditures and oversee business operations. The committee does not make football decisions, contrary to popular belief. Some committee members in recent years have pushed for the right to approve major trades because of their impact on the franchise as a business entity. The thinking is that this extra step would help prevent the team from mortgaging its future with a "panic" trade—such as the John Hadl deal under Dan Devine, or, more recently, the Minnesota Vikings' trade for Herschel Walker.

But that would seemingly contradict President Bob Harlan's philosophy of letting general manager Ron Wolf make all the football decisions. Besides, Wolf is too good a football man to make a trade that would threaten the future of the franchise.

Games on Sundays in Green Bay are events. Our fans drive here from Madison and Milwaukee, from La Crosse and Wausau, from Marquette, Mich., and even Chicago and Minneapolis. There is an electricity in the air that is impossible to describe. It's magical.

Another phenomenon of our small-town franchise is that we are a great draw on the road. In cities such as Los Angeles and Phoenix, the Packers have a huge and loyal following of relocated Wisconsinites.

And what is truly amazing about our fans is that they continued to support us through the 1970s and '80s, when we were mediocre at best, and at times downright pathetic. In all of professional sports, perhaps only baseball's Chicago Cubs can rival the Packers for retaining their fan base throughout a long drought.

In a spiritual but very real way, the Packers are loved in the 1990s because of what they accomplished in the '60s. There is no doubt that our championship seasons put us in the position we are in today. A good number of our fans grew up watching and cheering Paul Hornung, Ray Nitschke, and Bart Starr.

There is a faction that wants to bury the Glory Years in the history books, once and for all. They believe that by dwelling on the past, we aren't facing the reality of the present or preparing for the future.

I think that's hogwash. Let's face it: Vince Lombardi is still selling tickets for the Green Bay Packers.

It's been a long time since Vince shook my hand and told me, "I think you're my man." In the ensuing years, we won five league championships and the first two Super Bowls. In 1993, we became the first NFL team to mark its 75th season in the league.

And while all that was happening, Bart Starr turned into Lynn Dickey, who turned into Don Majkowski, who turned into Brett Favre.

For 32 years, I had the best seat in the house. There's no place on earth like the sideline at Lambeau Field on an clear, crisp autumn Sunday.

I've been blessed with a wonderful family, a great career, and a lifetime of memories.

And if I could be granted one more wish, it would be that the Packers make it back to the Super Bowl before I die. I would love to see the players holding aloft the aptly named Vince Lombardi Trophy.

It would be a closure of sorts for me, a completion of the circle.

And it would be the beginning for a whole new generation of Green Bay Packers fans.

What a wonderful thought.

About the Authors

DOMENIC GENTILE joined the Green Bay Packers on a part-time basis in 1961. After a five-minute interview, coach Vince Lombardi told Gentile, "I think you're my man." That was the beginning of a 32-year association with the Packers that spanned seven coaching staffs and 494 National Football League games. Gentile became the team's first full-time trainer in 1969 and retired following the 1992 season. Over the years, he taped Paul Hornung's ankles and Bart Starr's fragile shoulder, counseled the insecure Travis Williams and Chester Marcol and helped Jerry Kramer and Lynn Dickey rehabilitate their numerous injuries. The Professional Football Athletic Trainers Society honored Gentile and assistant Kurt Fielding as the NFL's Training Staff of the Year in 1992. Gentile served as an honorary captain for the Packers in their last game of the 1992 season. In April, 1993, Gentile was inducted into the Wisconsin Athletic Trainers Association Hall of Fame. In 1995, he was inducted into the Lakeshore All-Sports Hall of Fame in Manitowoc, the Wisconsin Hall of Fame in Eau Claire, the North Dakota State University Hall of Fame in Fargo, and the National Athletic Trainers Association Hall of Fame. He lives in De Pere, Wisconsin, with his wife, Peggy. The couple have four children—Annette Gulseth, Michael, Greg, and Marie Waldschmidt.

GARY D'AMATO has been a member of the *Milwaukee Journal Sentinel* sports staff since 1990. Prior to that, he was sports editor of the *Racine Journal Times,* for which he regularly covered the Packers. D'Amato has won more than 20 writing awards in his 17 years as a newspaper reporter, including first-place honors in the prestigious Associated Press Sports Editors contest, the Wisconsin Newspaper Association, and the Milwaukee Press Club. He lives in St. Francis, Wisconsin, with his wife, Dee Dee. The couple have three children: Nicole, Tarah, and Dean.